THE
ABUNDANCE FORMULA

9 PROVEN STEPS TO BUILD BLACK
FAMILY WEALTH, PROTECT
YOUR LEGACY,
AND EMPOWER GENERATIONS

BY ASH CASH &
AMINA PHELPS

All rights reserved under the international and Pan-American copyright conventions.

First published in the United States of America.

All rights reserved. With the exception of brief quotations in a review, no part of this book may be reproduced or transmitted, in any form, or by any means, electronic or mechanical (including photocopying), nor may it be stored in any information storage and retrieval system without written permission from the publisher.

DISCLAIMER

The advice contained in this material might not be suitable for everyone. The authors designed the information to present their opinion about the subject matter. The reader must carefully investigate all aspects of any business decision before committing to him or herself. The authors obtained the information contained herein from sources they believe to be reliable and from their own personal experience, but they neither imply nor intend any guarantee of accuracy. The authors are not in the business of giving legal, accounting, or any other type of professional advice. Should the reader need such advice, he or she must seek services from a competent professional. The authors particularly disclaims any liability, loss, or risk taken by individuals who directly or indirectly act on the information contained herein. The authors believe the advice presented here is sound, but readers cannot hold them responsible for either the actions they take, or the risk taken by individuals who directly or indirectly act on the information contained herein.

Published by 1BrickPublishing
Printed in the United States
Copyright © 2025 by Ash'Cash & Amina Phelps
ISBN 978-1949303841 (Print)
ISBN 978-1949303858 (Hardcover)
ISBN 978-1949303865 (E-Book)

DEDICATION

To the Black families across generations who have persevered against tremendous odds to build, protect, and pass down what they could—your resilience is the foundation upon which this work stands.

To our ancestors who planted seeds of economic wisdom they would never see bloom—we harvest the fruits of your sacrifice with deep gratitude.

To our children, grandchildren, and all future generations who will build upon what we establish today—may you find in these pages both practical tools and the unwavering belief that Abundance is Your Birthright.

And to our community—bound together not just by shared history but by shared destiny—may this work contribute to the collective prosperity that strengthens us all.

Because Black family unity is the foundation of Black wealth.

DEDICATION REQUEST

Please share this book with anyone who you feel would benefit from its guidance, inspiration, and actionable steps for unlocking the abundance that is rightfully theirs.

If this book empowers you on your wealth-building journey, consider it your responsibility to ensure its wisdom reaches others in our community. Pass it to the young entrepreneur seeking financial knowledge, the parents striving to create generational wealth, the professionals looking to align their success with community empowerment, or anyone committed to economic liberation.

True abundance multiplies when shared. Just as we must circulate our dollars within our community to build collective prosperity, so too must we circulate knowledge that creates the foundation for that prosperity.

When you share this book, you're not just passing along pages—you're extending an invitation to join a movement of families committed to creating lasting financial legacies.

TABLE OF CONTENTS

Introduction 1
Chapter 1: **A**lign Your Savings And Spending 9
Chapter 2: **B**roaden Your Earnings 27
Chapter 3: **U**nderwrite Your Financial Freedom Fund 59
Chapter 4: **N**urture Creditworthiness And Use Credit
To Build Wealth 91
Chapter 5: **D**iminish Liabilities 119
Chapter 6: **A**mplify Investments 153
Chapter 7: **N**avigate A Life Insurance Strategy 197
Chapter 8: **C**reate A Tax Wealth Strategy 235
Chapter 9: **E**stablish Legacy 281
Chapter 10: Empowering The Community 317
Conclusion: Living The Abundance Formula 355
Appendices 363
About The Authors 407
Index 409

INTRODUCTION

The Blueprint for Black Family Wealth

There's an old African proverb that says, "If you want to go fast, go alone. If you want to go far, go together." For us—Ash and Amina—this wisdom has been the cornerstone of not only our 20-year partnership in life and business but also our approach to wealth building. We've discovered that true abundance isn't achieved in isolation; it blooms through family unity, community support, and generational thinking.

A Divine Appointment

Some moments in life are so perfectly aligned that they can only be described as divine. For us, one such moment occurred when we had the extraordinary privilege of meeting Dr. Claud Anderson and his family. For years, we had studied Dr. Anderson's groundbreaking work, particularly his book *PowerNomics: The National Plan to Empower Black America*. His teachings on group economics, wealth building through community empowerment, and the critical importance of Black ownership resonated deeply with us.

What began as a professional engagement—we were tasked with helping Dr. Anderson transform *PowerNomics* into an audiobook—evolved into something much more profound. As we immersed ourselves in the project, working closely with the text and connecting with the Anderson family, we experienced a profound awakening. The depth and timelessness of Dr. Anderson's message struck us with renewed clarity and urgency. We realized that these principles needed to be carried forward, adapted for today's families, and integrated into practical, actionable strategies that could transform Black financial futures.

That divine appointment became our calling: to take the torch of *PowerNomics* and carry its flame into a new generation of wealth builders.

Standing on the Shoulders of Giants

Our approach to wealth building draws from two powerful traditions. First, the principles of *PowerNomics* provide the philosophical foundation—understanding that true empowerment for Black families must include economic self-sufficiency, group cooperation, and strategic resource management.

Second, we've studied the wealth-building practices of America's wealthiest families, particularly the Rockefellers, whose multigenerational wealth strategies have proven remarkably effective. In the illuminating book *What Would the Rockefellers Do?*, authors Garrett Gunderson and Michael Isom reveal how one of history's wealthiest families created systems that protected and grew their assets across generations. They mastered the art of using financial tools—like banking, insurance, and trusts—not as mere products but as strategic vehicles for wealth accumulation and preservation.

INTRODUCTION

We've taken these two powerful frameworks and integrated them into a comprehensive system that speaks directly to the unique challenges and opportunities facing Black families today. This isn't about merely copying the Rockefellers or rigidly applying every concept from *PowerNomics*. It's about intelligently adapting these proven principles to create a blueprint for Black family prosperity that acknowledges our history while boldly claiming our economic future.

Why This Book Now?

We live in a time of both unprecedented challenges and extraordinary opportunities for Black wealth creation. The wealth gap in America remains stark: according to the Federal Reserve, the typical White family has eight times the wealth of the typical Black family. This gap isn't merely about income—it's about assets, ownership, and financial literacy.

Yet simultaneously, we're witnessing a renaissance of Black entrepreneurship, increasing awareness about the importance of investing, and a growing movement toward economic solidarity within our communities. The time is ripe for a comprehensive guide that speaks specifically to Black families about building lasting wealth.

The Abundance Formula is more than a financial planning book. It's a response to generations of systematic economic exclusion. It's a roadmap for families who want to break cycles of financial struggle. It's a vision for how Black America can harness its tremendous economic power to create lasting prosperity.

The 9-Step ABUNDANCE Checklist

At the heart of this book is the Abundance Checklist—nine proven steps that, when implemented together, create a powerful ecosystem for wealth creation and preservation. These steps aren't arbitrary; they're based on the practices of wealthy families who have maintained their fortunes across generations, adapted specifically for the challenges and opportunities facing Black families today.

1. **Align Your Savings and Spending**: Before you can build wealth, you need to ensure your financial foundation is solid. We'll help you create a personal financial statement and align your spending with your values and goals.
2. **Broaden Your Earnings**: The average millionaire has seven streams of income. We'll guide you in diversifying your income sources to create stability and growth opportunities.
3. **Underwrite Your Financial Freedom Fund**: Financial security begins with having reserves to weather life's storms. We'll show you how to build and maintain this critical safety net.
4. **Nurture Creditworthiness**: Your credit score is more than a number—it's a powerful wealth-building tool when used strategically. We'll teach you how to maximize its potential.
5. **Diminish Liabilities**: Not all debt is created equal. Learn to eliminate wealth-draining liabilities while leveraging strategic debt to build assets.
6. **Amplify Investments**: Transform your earnings into assets that work for you. We'll explore strategies for stock market investing, real estate, business ownership, and more.

7. **N**avigate a Life Insurance Strategy: Discover how properly structured life insurance becomes not just protection but a powerful vehicle for tax-advantaged wealth building.
8. **C**reate a Tax Wealth Strategy: Keep more of what you earn by implementing legal tax strategies used by the wealthy for generations.
9. **E**stablish Legacy: Learn how to protect what you've built and ensure it benefits future generations through proper estate planning.

These nine steps are interconnected and mutually reinforcing. Throughout this book, you'll discover how implementing this system can transform not just your financial situation but your entire family's relationship with money and wealth.

Our Journey, Your Roadmap

As we share these principles with you, we do so not as distant experts but as practitioners who have walked this path ourselves. Before becoming financial educators, Ash spent 15 years in banking, working with some of America's wealthiest individuals and families. Amina has consulted with Fortune 500 companies, providing expertise in tax strategy and organizational leadership. Together, we've built multiple seven-figure businesses while raising our family with these same financial principles.

We've witnessed firsthand the transformative power of these strategies—not just in our lives but in the lives of the countless families we've had the privilege to guide. We've seen people go from paycheck-to-paycheck living to building significant net worth. We've helped entrepreneurs scale from side hustles to thriving businesses. We've guided families in creating estate plans that will benefit generations to come.

The path hasn't always been straight or easy. We've made mistakes, learned hard lessons, and continually refined our approach. This book represents the distillation of those experiences—the strategies that have proven most effective, the pitfalls to avoid, and the mindset shifts that make the biggest difference.

Beyond Individual Wealth: A Vision for Community Prosperity

While this book focuses on family wealth building, we never lose sight of Dr. Anderson's broader vision: collective economic empowerment for Black America. True prosperity isn't just about individual families becoming wealthy in isolation. It's about creating an ecosystem of Black wealth that strengthens our communities, funds our institutions, and creates opportunities for future generations.

Throughout this book, we'll explore how implementing the Abundance Formula in your family contributes to this larger vision. You'll discover opportunities to practice group economics by supporting Black businesses. You'll learn how your investment decisions can strengthen Black financial institutions. You'll see how creating generational wealth in your family contributes to narrowing the racial wealth gap for our entire community.

INTRODUCTION

How to Use This Book

The Abundance Formula is designed to be both inspirational and practical. In each chapter, we'll explore one of the nine steps in detail, providing both the conceptual understanding of why it matters and the practical steps for implementation.

You'll find:

- **Stories and case studies** from real families who have successfully implemented these strategies
- **Action steps** at the end of each chapter to help you apply what you've learned
- **Worksheets and planning tools** to guide your wealth-building journey
- **Resource recommendations** for further learning and support

We recommend reading the book from beginning to end first to understand how the nine steps work together as a system. Then, return to individual chapters as you implement each step in your own financial life.

Remember that wealth building is a journey, not a destination. The strategies in this book aren't about getting rich quick; they're about creating sustainable, multigenerational prosperity. Some steps you may be able to implement immediately, while others might be goals to work toward over time. That's perfectly normal and expected.

A New Legacy Begins Now

As we close this introduction, we want to acknowledge the weight and significance of this moment. By picking up this book, you've taken the first step toward creating a new financial legacy for your family—one of abundance, security, and empowerment.

The barriers to Black wealth have been many, from historical injustices to present-day inequities. But as Dr. Anderson taught us, the path forward isn't through victimhood but through strategic action. The Abundance Formula provides that strategy—a proven system for building wealth that honors our past while boldly claiming our economic future.

We are honored to walk this path with you. Let's begin.

With abundant blessings,

Ash Cash & Amina Phelps

CHAPTER 1

ALIGN YOUR SAVINGS AND SPENDING

> *"Do not save what is left after spending, but spend what is left after saving."*
> —Warren Buffett

"We don't have enough money to save." These words came from James and Tanya, a couple in their mid-thirties who reached out to us after attending one of our financial freedom workshops in Atlanta. They had good jobs—James as an IT specialist and Tanya as a nurse practitioner—with a combined income that put them firmly in the upper-middle class. They owned a beautiful home in a desirable suburb and drove newer model cars. From the outside looking in, they appeared to be living the American dream.

But behind closed doors, the reality was starkly different. Despite earning well over six figures combined, they found themselves living paycheck to paycheck. Credit card debt had slowly accumulated to nearly $30,000. Their mortgage payment, coupled with car loans and student debt, consumed most of their monthly income. They had less than $5,000 in savings. Retirement accounts were minimal. The stress of their financial situation was taking a toll on their relationship and their health.

"Where does all the money go?" James asked during our first meeting, genuine confusion in his voice.

Their situation isn't unique. In fact, it's distressingly common. According to Federal Reserve data, nearly 40% of American adults would struggle to cover an unexpected $400 expense. Among Black households specifically, the median family savings is dramatically lower than the national average, making financial emergencies particularly devastating.

What James and Tanya discovered—and what you might recognize in your own life—is that income alone doesn't create wealth. Even high earners can find themselves financially vulnerable if their spending isn't aligned with their long-term goals. This misalignment is the first barrier to building real wealth, and it's why "Align Your Savings and Spending" is step one in our Abundance Formula.

Understanding Your Financial Alignment

Think of financial alignment as the foundation upon which your wealth is built. Just like a house with a weak foundation will eventually develop cracks and instability, a financial life with misaligned savings and spending patterns will never support lasting wealth.

Alignment happens when your spending decisions reflect your values and long-term goals rather than temporary desires or social pressures. It means having clarity about where your money is going and why it's going there. Most importantly, it means prioritizing your financial future by paying yourself first through consistent saving and investing.

For many Black families, achieving this alignment is complicated by unique cultural and historical factors. Centuries of economic exclusion and discrimination have created what financial psychologists call "money trauma"—anxiety, fear, and dysfunctional behaviors around money that can be passed down through generations. Add to this the pressure to "look successful" through visible status symbols and the genuine desire to give our children opportunities we may not have had, and the result can be spending patterns that undermine our long-term financial health.

The good news? Financial alignment is a skill that can be learned, practiced, and mastered. It starts with understanding where you are now.

The Personal Financial Statement: Your Financial Truth

When working with James and Tanya, our first step was creating a personal financial statement—a comprehensive snapshot of their current financial position. This document isn't just about tracking expenses; it's about facing financial reality with complete honesty.

A personal financial statement consists of two key components:

1. **Net Worth Statement:** A listing of everything you own (assets) minus everything you owe (liabilities).
2. **Cash Flow Statement:** A detailed record of your income and expenses over a specific period.

Together, these documents tell the story of your financial life. They reveal patterns, highlight problems, and provide the clarity needed to make meaningful changes.

Let's start with creating your own Personal Financial Statement.

Building Your Net Worth Statement

Your net worth is the most important number in your financial life. It's calculated using a simple formula:

Assets - Liabilities = Net Worth

Assets are things you own that have value, such as:

- Cash in checking and savings accounts
- Investments (stocks, bonds, mutual funds, etc.)
- Real estate (your home, investment properties)
- Personal property (vehicles, jewelry, furniture, etc.)
- Business interests
- Retirement accounts (401(k), IRA, etc.)

Liabilities are what you owe:

- Mortgage balance
- Car loans
- Student loans
- Credit card balances
- Personal loans
- Medical debt
- Other obligations

To create your net worth statement:

1. List all your assets and their current market values
2. List all your liabilities and their current balances
3. Subtract the total liabilities from the total assets

This calculation will give you your current net worth—a number that may be positive, negative, or close to zero. Whatever the result, don't judge yourself. This is simply your starting point, and knowing it is powerful.

For James and Tanya, this exercise was eye-opening. Despite their high incomes, their net worth was just $43,000—primarily the small amount of equity they had in their home after years of mortgage payments. Their cars, which they considered assets, were actually liabilities due to their outstanding auto loans. Their substantial student loans further reduced their net worth.

"I thought we were doing better than this," Tanya admitted quietly.

That moment of realization, though painful, became their turning point. Knowing their true financial position allowed them to make informed decisions about their future.

Creating Your Cash Flow Statement

While your net worth tells you where you stand right now, your cash flow statement reveals how you got there and where you're headed. It tracks money flowing in (income) and money flowing out (expenses) over time.

To create your cash flow statement:

1. Record all sources of income (salary, bonuses, side hustles, investments, etc.)
2. Track all expenses, categorized by type (housing, transportation, food, entertainment, etc.)
3. Calculate the difference (income minus expenses)

This difference—your cash flow margin—determines whether you're building wealth or falling behind. A positive margin means you're spending less than you earn, creating the opportunity to save and invest. A negative margin means you're spending more than you earn, likely accumulating debt.

For many families, tracking expenses reveals surprising patterns. James and Tanya discovered they were spending over $1,200 monthly on restaurants and food delivery—far more than they realized. They found numerous subscription services they rarely used, impulse purchases that added no real value to their lives, and significant money spent on convenience items that could easily be eliminated.

"We've been bleeding money without even knowing it," James said.

This clarity about where their money was going empowered them to make intentional changes. And this is where the real work of alignment begins.

Setting SMART Financial Goals

With a clear understanding of your current financial position, the next step is defining where you want to go. Financial goals provide direction and purpose to your money decisions. Without them, it's easy to drift along, responding to whatever financial pressures arise in the moment.

The most effective financial goals follow the SMART framework:

- **Specific:** Clearly defined and precise
- **Measurable:** Quantifiable so you can track progress
- **Achievable:** Realistic given your resources and constraints
- **Relevant:** Aligned with your values and long-term aspirations
- **Timebound:** Attached to a specific deadline or timeframe

For example, rather than setting a vague goal like "save more money," a SMART goal would be: "Save $10,000 for an emergency fund by December 31, 2026, by automatically transferring $850 per month to a high-yield savings account."

Financial goals typically fall into three timeframes:

1. **Short-term goals** (under 1 year): Building an emergency fund, paying off a credit card, saving for a vacation
2. **Mid-term goals** (1-5 years): Down payment on a home, starting a business, major home renovations
3. **Long-term goals** (5+ years): Retirement, children's college education, generational wealth transfer

James and Tanya worked to establish goals in each category:

- Short-term: Build a $20,000 emergency fund within 12 months
- Mid-term: Pay off all credit card debt ($30,000) within 2 years
- Long-term: Fully fund their retirement accounts and establish a college fund for their infant daughter

With these clearly defined targets, they could now align their spending decisions with their priorities.

The Power of Intentional Spending

The heart of financial alignment is intentional spending—making conscious choices about where your money goes based on your values and goals rather than impulse, emotion, or social pressure.

Intentional spending doesn't mean never enjoying your money. It means ensuring that every dollar serves a purpose you've thoughtfully chosen. It's about quality over quantity, value over status, and long-term satisfaction over momentary pleasure.

For Black families, intentional spending often means confronting and rejecting harmful narratives about consumption and success. We've been bombarded with messages that equate worth with possessions, that promote a "ball out" mentality, and that encourage using material goods to compensate for historical exclusion. Rejecting these narratives is an act of financial and cultural empowerment.

To practice intentional spending:

1. **Identify your true values.** What matters most to you? Family security? Creative expression? Community impact? Education? Freedom and flexibility? The answers will be different for everyone, but they should guide your financial decisions.
2. **Question every expenditure.** Before making significant purchases, ask yourself: Does this align with my values and goals?

Will this bring lasting satisfaction? Is this the best use of my financial resources?

3. **Implement the 24-hour rule.** For non-essential purchases over a certain amount (say, $100), wait 24 hours before buying. This creates space for the initial emotional response to subside, allowing for more rational decision-making.
4. **Practice gratitude for what you already have.** Research shows that gratitude reduces the impulse to acquire more possessions. Regularly reflect on and appreciate what you already own.
5. **Find non-monetary ways to meet emotional needs.** Often, impulse spending is an attempt to fulfill emotional needs like connection, excitement, or security. Explore non-financial ways to meet these needs.

For James and Tanya, intentional spending meant realigning their lifestyle with their long-term goals. They didn't stop eating out entirely, but they reduced it to once a week as a special family occasion rather than a daily convenience. They traded their luxury cars for reliable but less expensive models, eliminating their car payments. They canceled unused subscriptions and memberships.

These changes weren't sacrifices but reallocations. Every dollar saved from these areas went directly toward their goals—building their emergency fund, eliminating credit card debt, and investing for their daughter's future.

The Pay Yourself First Principle

At the core of financial alignment is the "pay yourself first" principle—the practice of automatically directing a portion of your income to savings and investments before paying bills or making discretionary purchases.

This approach inverts the traditional pattern of: Income → Bills → Discretionary Spending → Saving (if anything's left)

To the wealth-building pattern of: Income → Saving/Investing → Bills → Discretionary Spending

This simple reordering makes a profound difference. It transforms saving from an afterthought to a priority, ensuring that wealth-building happens consistently regardless of other financial pressures.

For James and Tanya, implementing this principle meant setting up automatic transfers on payday:

- 10% of their income went directly to retirement accounts
- 5% went to their emergency fund
- 5% went to their debt payoff fund
- The remaining 80% covered their living expenses and obligations

Within six months, they had accumulated over $12,000 in their emergency fund. Within a year, they had paid off half their credit card debt. Their net worth began to grow steadily, and their financial stress noticeably decreased.

"For the first time, I feel like we're in control of our money, not the other way around," Tanya shared.

Creating Your Aligned Budget

With clear financial goals and a commitment to intentional spending, the next step is creating a budget that reflects these priorities. An aligned budget isn't about restriction—it's about allocation. It ensures your money flows toward what matters most to you.

The most effective budgeting approach for building wealth is the percentage-based budget, which divides your income into broad categories:

- **50% for Needs:** Housing, utilities, groceries, transportation, minimum debt payments, basic insurances
- **30% for Wants:** Dining out, entertainment, travel, hobbies, clothing beyond the basics
- **20% for Wealth Building:** Saving, investing, additional debt payments, giving

These percentages can be adjusted based on your specific situation and goals. For example, if building wealth quickly is your priority, you might allocate 30% to wealth building and reduce your wants to 20%.

For families in high-cost areas, the needs category might need to be higher initially. The key is to find a sustainable balance that allows you to meet your obligations while consistently moving toward your financial goals.

James and Tanya adapted this framework to their situation:

- 55% for Needs (they lived in an expensive area)

- 20% for Wants (they reduced this category to accelerate debt payoff)
- 25% for Wealth Building (split between emergency fund, debt payoff, and retirement)

Within each category, they allocated specific amounts to different expenses. This wasn't a rigid prison but a flexible framework that evolved as their circumstances changed. When they received raises or bonuses, the additional money went primarily to wealth building rather than lifestyle inflation.

Overcoming Common Barriers to Financial Alignment

The path to financial alignment isn't always smooth. Several common barriers can derail even the best intentions:

1. Income Volatility

For entrepreneurs, freelancers, commission-based workers, and many others, income fluctuates month to month. This variability can make consistent saving and budgeting challenging.

Solution: Build your financial plan around your baseline income—the minimum you can reliably expect each month. Treat any income above this baseline as a bonus allocated primarily to wealth building. Additionally, aim to build a larger emergency fund (9-12 months of expenses rather than the standard 3-6 months) to buffer against income fluctuations.

2. Financial Support to Extended Family

Many Black professionals find themselves supporting extended family members financially—sometimes called the "Black tax." While family support is deeply valued in our community, it can impede personal wealth building if not managed thoughtfully.

Solution: Include family support in your budget as a planned expense rather than an emergency drain. Set clear boundaries about what you can sustainably provide. Consider non-monetary ways to support family, such as helping them access resources, education, or opportunities. Remember that building your own wealth ultimately increases your capacity to help others.

3. Past Financial Mistakes

Previous financial errors can create both practical barriers (poor credit, debt) and psychological barriers (shame, fear, avoidance) to financial progress.

Solution: Address the practical consequences methodically through debt management strategies and credit rebuilding. Process the emotional aspects by recognizing that past mistakes don't define your financial future. Practice self-compassion while taking responsibility for moving forward differently.

4. Lifestyle Expectations

Social and cultural pressures can create expectations about how you should live and what you should own, often at odds with wealth-building priorities.

Solution: Clarify your personal values and priorities. Practice the art of saying "not right now" to expenditures that don't align with your goals. Find communities that support your financial journey rather than pressuring you toward unsustainable spending.

5. Lack of Financial Knowledge

Many of us didn't receive comprehensive financial education growing up, making it difficult to navigate complex financial decisions confidently.

Solution: Commit to ongoing financial education through books, courses, podcasts, and mentorship. Remember that financial literacy is a journey, not a destination. Be patient with yourself as you learn and implement new concepts.

Your Financial Alignment Action Plan

Now it's time to put these principles into action. Here's a step-by-step plan to align your savings and spending with your wealth-building goals:

- ☐ **Create your personal financial statement**
    - ☐ Calculate your current net worth
    - ☐ Track your income and expenses for at least one month
    - ☐ Identify areas of financial strength and weakness

- [ ] **Establish your SMART financial goals**
  - [ ] Define short-term, mid-term, and long-term objectives
  - [ ] Ensure each goal is specific, measurable, achievable, relevant, and timebound
  - [ ] Write these goals down and place them where you'll see them regularly
- [ ] **Implement a "pay yourself first" system**
  - [ ] Open dedicated accounts for different goals if you haven't already
  - [ ] Set up automatic transfers on payday to your savings and investment accounts
  - [ ] Start with whatever percentage feels manageable, even if it's just 1-2%
- [ ] **Create your aligned budget**
  - [ ] Allocate your income into needs, wants, and wealth-building categories
  - [ ] Make specific allocations within each category
  - [ ] Track your spending against these allocations
- [ ] **Practice intentional spending**
  - [ ] Implement the 24-hour rule for non-essential purchases
  - [ ] Question expenditures against your values and goals
  - [ ] Find non-monetary ways to fulfill emotional needs
- [ ] **Review and adjust regularly**
  - [ ] Schedule monthly financial check-ins with yourself (and your partner if applicable)
  - [ ] Track your progress toward goals
  - [ ] Make adjustments as your income, expenses, and priorities evolve

James and Tanya: Three Years Later

Remember James and Tanya from the beginning of this chapter? Let's check in on their progress three years after implementing these principles.

Their financial transformation has been remarkable:

- Their emergency fund now stands at $30,000—six months of living expenses
- All credit card debt has been eliminated
- Their net worth has grown to over $200,000
- They're maxing out their retirement accounts
- Their daughter's college fund has over $15,000
- They've started a small real estate investment portfolio

Most importantly, they've broken free from financial stress and anxiety. They sleep better at night. They argue less about money. They feel empowered rather than overwhelmed.

"The most surprising thing," James reflected, "is that we don't feel deprived. We're actually enjoying life more because we're not constantly worried about money. We still do the things that matter to us—we just do them more intentionally."

Tanya added, "And we're teaching our daughter healthy money habits from the beginning. That's a gift our parents couldn't give us because they didn't have it themselves."

This is the power of financial alignment—it creates not just wealth but wellbeing. It establishes not just financial security but freedom. It builds not just individual prosperity but generational transformation.

CHAPTER 1: ALIGN YOUR SAVINGS AND SPENDING

Your Journey Begins Here

As we close this chapter, remember that financial alignment is not about perfection but progress. It's about making incremental improvements that compound over time. Every positive financial decision, no matter how small, moves you closer to your goals.

The journey to family wealth begins with this first step—aligning what you earn with what you truly value. When your spending reflects your priorities and your saving becomes automatic, you create the foundation upon which all other wealth-building efforts will rest.

In the next chapter, we'll explore how to expand your income through multiple streams, accelerating your path to abundance. But first, complete the action steps below to solidify your financial alignment.

ACTION STEP: Draft a Budget Aligned with Your Goals and Lifestyle Aspirations

- ☐ **Complete your personal financial statement**
    - ☐ List all assets and their values
    - ☐ List all liabilities and their balances
    - ☐ Calculate your current net worth
    - ☐ Track your income and expenses for one month
- ☐ **Define your financial goals**
    - ☐ Short-term (under 1 year)
    - ☐ Mid-term (1-5 years)

- [ ] Long-term (5+ years)
- [ ] **Create your percentage-based budget**
    - [ ] Allocate percentages to needs, wants, and wealth building
    - [ ] Make specific allocations within each category
    - [ ] Identify areas to reduce in order to increase wealth building
- [ ] **Set up automatic transfers**
    - [ ] Open dedicated accounts for different goals if needed
    - [ ] Schedule transfers to occur on payday
    - [ ] Start with whatever percentage is sustainable
- [ ] **Schedule your first monthly financial review**
    - [ ] Put a recurring appointment on your calendar
    - [ ] Prepare to track progress toward goals
    - [ ] Plan to make adjustments as needed

Remember: Financial alignment is a practice, not a one-time event. Be patient with yourself as you develop new habits and systems.

CHAPTER 2

BROADEN YOUR EARNINGS

"Don't put all your eggs in one basket."
—Ancient Proverb

Marcus was raised to believe that success meant one thing: getting a good education, finding a stable job with benefits, and climbing the corporate ladder. His parents—his father a postal worker for 32 years and his mother an elementary school teacher—had instilled in him the value of job security. They had lived through layoffs and economic downturns that devastated friends and family who didn't have stable government jobs, and they wanted better for their son.

Marcus followed their advice perfectly. He earned his bachelor's degree in business administration, then an MBA. He landed a management position at a Fortune 500 company with an excellent salary and benefits package. He worked diligently, earned promotions, and by his mid-thirties was making well into six figures.

Then came the corporate restructuring. Despite his performance and dedication, Marcus found himself among the thousands laid off as the company outsourced much of its middle management. His severance package was generous—six months of salary—but the job market had changed dramatically. Companies were hiring contractors rather than employees, automation had eliminated many positions, and his specialized skills didn't transfer easily to other industries.

"I did everything right," Marcus told us during our first consultation, frustration evident in his voice. "I got the education, put in the hours, played by the rules. And now I'm starting over at 38."

Marcus's story highlights a critical truth that many Black professionals are discovering: relying on a single source of income—no matter how substantial or seemingly secure—is increasingly risky in today's economy. This reality is why "Broaden Your Earnings" is the second step in our Abundance Formula.

The Myth of Job Security

For generations, Black families have emphasized education and stable employment as the path to financial security. This emphasis made perfect sense historically. When our grandparents and parents entered the workforce, many companies still offered lifetime employment, pension plans, and predictable career paths. Government jobs provided reliable incomes with excellent benefits and protection from discrimination that was rampant in the private sector.

This focus on stable employment was also a logical response to the economic discrimination Black Americans faced. When banking, real estate, and business opportunities were systematically denied to us, a good job with regular pay represented the most accessible path to financial stability.

But the economic landscape has fundamentally changed:

- The average person now changes jobs 12 times during their career
- Traditional pension plans have largely been replaced by self-funded retirement accounts
- Technological advancement and automation continue to eliminate entire categories of jobs
- Globalization has shifted millions of positions overseas
- The gig economy has transformed many full-time roles into contract positions

These shifts have created a new reality: job security is largely an illusion. Even the most stable-seeming positions can disappear overnight due to factors entirely outside an individual's control—corporate mergers, technological disruption, economic downturns, or changing market conditions.

This reality doesn't mean education and employment aren't valuable—they absolutely are. But relying exclusively on a single paycheck creates vulnerability, regardless of how impressive that paycheck might be.

The 7 Streams of Income Strategy

Research has consistently shown that the average millionaire has seven streams of income. This diversification creates resilience, opportunity, and accelerated wealth-building potential. When one stream faces challenges, others continue flowing; when one presents unexpected opportunities, you have the resources to capitalize on them.

The seven types of income streams typically include:

1. **Earned Income:** Salary from employment or self-employment
2. **Business Income:** Profits from businesses you own (fully or partially)
3. **Interest Income:** Money earned from saving accounts, CDs, bonds, etc.
4. **Dividend Income:** Payments received as a shareholder in profitable companies
5. **Rental Income:** Money earned from leasing property to others
6. **Capital Gains:** Profit from the sale of appreciated assets
7. **Royalty/Licensing Income:** Payment for use of something you created or own

For Black families building wealth, developing multiple income streams isn't just about financial optimization—it's about economic self-determination and resilience against biased systems. It's about creating options and opportunities for ourselves rather than depending on institutions that have historically excluded us.

Let's explore how to develop each of these income streams, with practical steps you can take regardless of your current financial situation.

Stream 1: Maximizing Your Earned Income

For most people, earned income from a job or career is the foundation upon which other income streams are built. Before diversifying, it's essential to maximize this primary source.

CHAPTER 2: BROADEN YOUR EARNINGS

Strategic Career Management

Rather than passively moving through your career, take an active role in managing it:

1. **Continuously develop in-demand skills.** Research which skills command premium salaries in your industry and invest in acquiring them through courses, certifications, or on-the-job experience.
2. **Master the art of negotiation.** Studies show that Black professionals, especially women, face significant biases in salary negotiation. Counter this by:
    - Researching industry salary standards thoroughly
    - Documenting your achievements and contributions quantitatively
    - Practicing negotiation scenarios with trusted mentors
    - Being prepared to walk away from undervalued offers
3. **Cultivate a strong professional network.** Your network often determines which opportunities you access. Attend industry events, join professional organizations, maintain relationships with former colleagues, and seek mentorship from successful professionals in your field.
4. **Position yourself for advancement.** Volunteer for high-visibility projects, seek feedback regularly, and ensure decision-makers are aware of your contributions and aspirations.
5. **Consider strategic job changes.** Staying at one company too long often results in below-market compensation. Research shows that changing employers every 3-5 years can increase lifetime earnings by 50% or more.

For Marcus, strategic career management meant broadening his skill set beyond his specific industry to include project management certification and digital marketing expertise. These transferable skills expanded his employability across sectors and ultimately helped him secure a new position with greater stability.

Income Stacking

Income stacking involves combining multiple part-time or flexible roles to create a full-time income that exceeds what you might earn in a single position. This approach works especially well for people with diverse skills and interests.

Examples include:

- A teacher who tutors privately after school and sells curriculum materials online
- A healthcare worker who picks up weekend shifts at different facilities and consults for healthcare technology companies
- An accountant who prepares taxes seasonally, bookkeeps for small businesses, and teaches financial literacy workshops

Income stacking creates natural income diversification while allowing you to explore different interests and develop various skills. It also provides flexibility that traditional full-time employment doesn't offer.

CHAPTER 2: BROADEN YOUR EARNINGS

Stream 2: Building Business Income

Business ownership has historically been one of the most powerful wealth-building tools, and it remains so today. The business income stream can take many forms, from full-time entrepreneurship to part-time side hustles.

Side Hustle Strategies

Starting a side business while maintaining your primary employment offers the best of both worlds: stable income plus entrepreneurial opportunity. Effective side hustles typically leverage:

1. **Existing skills and expertise.** What do you already know how to do well that others would pay for?
2. **Minimal startup costs.** Focus on businesses that require more effort than capital to launch.
3. **Flexible time commitments.** Choose ventures that can adapt to your available hours.
4. **Scalability potential.** Seek opportunities that could eventually grow into full-time businesses if successful.

Promising side hustle opportunities for Black entrepreneurs include:

- **Service-based businesses:** Consulting, coaching, tutoring, personal training, event planning, catering, photography, graphic design, writing, editing, virtual assistance
- **E-commerce:** Dropshipping, print-on-demand merchandise, handcrafted products, curated subscription boxes

- **Digital products:** Online courses, e-books, templates, planners, printables, stock photography, music, apps
- **Content creation:** YouTube channels, podcasts, blogs with affiliate marketing or advertising
- **Specialized marketplaces:** Etsy for crafts, Teachers Pay Teachers for educational materials, Fiverr for freelance services

When developing your side hustle, start small and focus on validating your business concept before investing significant time or money. Aim to secure your first paying customer as quickly as possible—this provides concrete feedback about whether your offering meets a real market need.

For Alicia, a corporate marketing executive we worked with, her passion for natural hair care became a successful side hustle selling handcrafted products online. She started with just five products made in her kitchen on weekends. Within two years, her "side hustle" was generating more income than her corporate salary, allowing her to transition to full-time entrepreneurship.

Strategic Business Selection

If you're considering full-time entrepreneurship, choosing the right type of business is crucial. Dr. Claud Anderson emphasized in PowerNomics that Black entrepreneurs should prioritize businesses that:

1. **Meet the needs of the Black community first.** What products or services do Black consumers currently purchase from non-Black businesses that you could provide instead?
2. **Can expand beyond the Black community.** While serving our community creates a strong foundation, the ability

to eventually expand to broader markets increases growth potential.
3. **Utilize our cultural competitive advantages.** In what areas do we have cultural insights, expertise, or credibility that others lack?
4. **Create jobs within the Black community.** Businesses that employ others multiply their economic impact.
5. **Can be vertically integrated.** Businesses that control multiple stages of their value chain retain more profit and build greater resilience.

Promising sectors for Black business ownership include:

- **Health and beauty:** Hair care, skincare, cosmetics, wellness products
- **Food and beverage:** Restaurants, catering, specialty food products, meal delivery
- **Media and entertainment:** Production companies, publishing, streaming platforms
- **Professional services:** Law, accounting, consulting, marketing, technology
- **Real estate and construction:** Development, property management, contracting, interior design
- **Education and childcare:** Private schools, tutoring centers, educational resources
- **Financial services:** Financial planning, insurance, tax preparation, bookkeeping

Whatever business you choose, focus on developing systems that eventually allow it to operate without your constant presence. A business dependent on your daily involvement isn't truly an asset—it's another job. True business income comes from enterprises that can generate profit whether you're personally present or not.

Business Acquisition vs. Startup

Starting a business from scratch isn't the only path to business ownership. Acquiring an existing business often presents less risk and faster returns than building one from nothing.

Consider these acquisition opportunities:

1. **Owner retirement:** Many baby boomer business owners are reaching retirement age without succession plans. They often sell at reasonable prices to buyers committed to continuing their legacy.
2. **Distressed businesses:** Companies facing temporary challenges can sometimes be purchased at significant discounts and turned around with fresh energy and perspective.
3. **Franchise opportunities:** Franchises offer established business models, training, and support systems that increase success probability.
4. **Partner buyouts:** Joining an existing business as a partner with an eventual buy-out agreement can create a smoother transition to ownership.

When Marcus's corporate job disappeared, he used part of his severance package to purchase a small digital marketing agency from a retiring owner. The business had stable clients and proven systems but needed modernization. Marcus's corporate experience and fresh perspective revitalized the agency, which now provides him with both personal income and business profit—two separate income streams.

Stream 3: Building Interest Income

Interest income—money earned from lending your capital to others—is one of the most passive income streams available. While today's low interest rate environment has diminished returns compared to previous generations, this income stream still plays an important role in a diversified income portfolio.

Strategic Interest Income Sources

Consider these options for generating interest income:

1. **High-yield savings accounts:** While traditional savings accounts offer minimal returns, online banks often provide higher yields with equal safety and FDIC insurance.
2. **Certificates of Deposit (CDs):** These time-limited deposits generally offer higher rates than savings accounts in exchange for committing your funds for a specific period (typically 3 months to 5 years).
3. **Money market accounts:** These hybrid accounts typically offer better rates than standard savings while maintaining liquidity and safety.
4. **Bonds:** Government and corporate bonds essentially loan your money to these entities in exchange for regular interest payments and eventual return of principal.

5. **Peer-to-peer lending:** Platforms like Prosper and LendingClub allow you to loan money directly to individuals, often at higher rates than traditional interest-bearing accounts (though with higher risk).
6. **Private lending:** Direct loans to individuals or businesses you know personally can generate substantial interest income, though they require careful documentation and risk assessment.

While interest rates on many of these vehicles remain relatively low, they serve important functions in your income strategy:

- Providing truly passive income
- Preserving capital while generating some return
- Creating liquidity for emergencies and opportunities
- Balancing riskier investments in your portfolio

The CD Ladder Strategy

To maximize returns while maintaining flexibility, consider implementing a CD ladder:

1. Divide your available funds into equal portions
2. Purchase CDs with different maturity dates (3 months, 6 months, 1 year, etc.)
3. When each CD matures, roll it into a new CD at the longest term in your ladder
4. Eventually, you'll have higher-yielding long-term CDs regularly maturing, providing both optimal returns and periodic access to your funds

This strategy works particularly well for emergency funds beyond your immediate needs and for short-to-medium term goals.

Stream 4: Building Dividend Income

Dividend income—regular payments made to shareholders of profitable companies—represents one of the most accessible passive income streams for average investors. Unlike interest income, dividend income often grows over time as companies increase their dividend payments and as you reinvest those dividends to purchase additional shares.

Dividend Investment Strategies

Consider these approaches to building dividend income:

1. **Dividend growth investing:** Focus on companies with histories of consistently raising their dividends year after year. These "Dividend Aristocrats" (companies that have increased dividends for at least 25 consecutive years) often provide reliable income that outpaces inflation.
2. **High-yield dividend investing:** Target companies paying above-average current dividend yields, typically 4-6%. While these may offer less dividend growth potential, they provide stronger immediate income.
3. **Dividend ETFs and mutual funds:** Instead of selecting individual dividend stocks, invest in funds that hold diversified portfolios of dividend-paying companies, providing instant diversification and professional management.

4. **REITs (Real Estate Investment Trusts):** These special investment vehicles are required to distribute 90% of their taxable income to shareholders, often resulting in above-average dividend yields while providing exposure to real estate markets.
5. **Preferred stocks:** These hybrid securities typically offer higher fixed dividend rates than common stocks, though with less potential for capital appreciation.

For maximum effectiveness, consider holding dividend investments in tax-advantaged accounts like Roth IRAs when possible, as this can eliminate taxes on both the dividends and their growth when withdrawn in retirement.

The Dividend Reinvestment Strategy

To accelerate your dividend income stream, implement a dividend reinvestment plan (DRIP):

1. Start with an initial investment in quality dividend-paying stocks or funds
2. Automatically reinvest all dividends to purchase additional shares
3. Make regular new contributions to your dividend portfolio
4. Allow compounding to work its magic over time

This strategy creates a snowball effect. As your reinvested dividends purchase more shares, those additional shares generate more dividends, which buy more shares, and so on. While the income stream starts small, it can grow substantially over time without requiring active management.

Marcus implemented this strategy after rebuilding his emergency fund. He dedicated 30% of his monthly investment budget specifically to dividend-focused ETFs. While the initial income was modest (about $50 monthly), he understood that consistent investment and reinvestment would compound over time to create a significant passive income stream.

Stream 5: Building Rental Income

Real estate has created more millionaires than perhaps any other asset class, and rental income represents one of its most powerful wealth-building mechanisms. For Black families in particular, real estate ownership offers both income potential and a stake in communities that have historically excluded us through discriminatory practices.

Rental Property Strategies

Consider these approaches to generating rental income:

1. **Single-family homes:** These typically offer the lowest barrier to entry for new real estate investors. They're easier to finance, manage, and sell than larger properties, making them ideal starting points.
2. **Multi-family properties:** Duplexes, triplexes, and small apartment buildings provide economies of scale—one roof, one tax bill, one insurance policy—but multiple rental incomes.
3. **House hacking:** Purchase a multi-unit property, live in one unit, and rent out the others. This allows your tenants to essentially cover your housing expenses while you build equity.

4. **Short-term rentals:** Platforms like Airbnb and VRBO enable property owners to generate premium returns compared to traditional long-term rentals, though with more active management requirements.
5. **Commercial real estate:** Retail spaces, office buildings, and industrial properties typically offer longer leases and less management intensity than residential rentals, though they require more capital and expertise.
6. **Real estate syndications:** These pooled investments allow you to participate in larger commercial properties alongside other investors, providing passive income without management responsibilities.
7. **Room rentals:** If you own your home, renting individual rooms can generate income without requiring additional property purchases.

The BRRRR strategy (Buy, Rehabilitate, Rent, Refinance, Repeat) offers a systematic approach to building a rental portfolio without continually investing new capital:

1. Buy undervalued properties needing improvement
2. Rehabilitate them to increase their value and rental potential
3. Rent them to quality tenants at market rates
4. Refinance to pull out your original investment (and often more)
5. Repeat the process with your recovered capital

This strategy allows you to potentially build a portfolio of cash-flowing properties while recycling the same initial investment capital.

CHAPTER 2: BROADEN YOUR EARNINGS

Alternative Real Estate Income Strategies

If traditional rental property ownership doesn't align with your resources or goals, consider these alternative approaches:

1. **Real Estate Investment Trusts (REITs):** These publicly traded companies own and manage income-producing real estate. Investing in REITs provides exposure to real estate markets without requiring property management or large capital investments.
2. **Real estate crowdfunding:** Platforms like Fundrise, RealtyMogul, and others allow you to invest in specific real estate projects with minimum investments as low as $500, providing access to commercial-scale opportunities previously available only to wealthy investors.
3. **Real estate notes:** Purchasing existing mortgages (often at a discount) allows you to collect the payments without owning the physical property.
4. **Tax lien investing:** Purchasing property tax liens from local governments can provide either interest income (when the property owner pays their delinquent taxes) or property acquisition (if they don't) at significant discounts.
5. **Property management:** If you have real estate expertise but limited capital, managing properties for others can generate income while building relationships and knowledge for future ownership.

Whatever approach you choose, remember that real estate investing is both a business and an investment. Success requires education, careful analysis, and systematic processes—not emotional decisions or get-rich-quick expectations.

Stream 6: Building Capital Gains Income

Capital gains—profit from selling assets that have appreciated in value—represent a powerful wealth-building stream that can create both regular income and substantial windfalls. While often associated with investment markets, capital gains opportunities exist in numerous asset categories.

Capital Gains Strategies

Consider these approaches to generating capital gains:

1. **Long-term equity investing:** Purchasing quality stocks, ETFs, or mutual funds and holding them through market cycles often produces significant capital appreciation over time. The S&P 500 has historically returned around 10% annually on average despite short-term volatility.
2. **Real estate appreciation:** Beyond rental income, real estate typically appreciates over time. Strategic improvements and neighborhood selection can accelerate this appreciation.
3. **Business building and selling:** Creating or purchasing businesses, improving their operations and profitability, then selling them to larger companies or investors can generate substantial capital gains.
4. **Personal property with appreciation potential:** Certain collectibles, art, vintage vehicles, limited-edition items, and

other tangible assets can significantly appreciate over time if carefully selected.
5. **Cryptocurrency and digital assets:** While highly volatile, cryptocurrencies and NFTs (non-fungible tokens) have created substantial capital gains for some investors, though they require risk tolerance and specialized knowledge.
6. **Private equity and venture capital:** Investing in early-stage companies, either directly or through funds, creates potential for significant capital gains when these companies grow or are acquired.

The most effective capital gains strategy typically involves patience and selectivity—identifying undervalued assets with strong appreciation potential, acquiring them at favorable prices, improving them when possible, and selling when their value has significantly increased.

Strategic Capital Gains Harvesting

To optimize capital gains as an income stream, consider implementing a strategic harvesting approach:

1. Maintain a diversified portfolio of appreciating assets acquired over different time periods
2. Establish value targets or holding periods for each asset
3. Systematically sell assets that have met their targets
4. Reinvest a portion of the proceeds into new appreciation opportunities
5. Direct another portion to income-producing assets
6. Reserve a final portion for personal use (your income)

This approach creates a repeatable cycle that generates periodic income while maintaining growth potential. It works particularly well when coordinated with tax planning strategies that minimize capital gains taxes through timing, offsetting gains with losses, and utilizing available exemptions.

After his layoff experience, Marcus implemented this strategy by allocating 20% of his monthly investment budget to growth-focused ETFs with the explicit intention of periodically selling portions of his appreciated investments to fund specific financial goals and supplement his income.

Stream 7: Building Royalty/Licensing Income

Royalty income—payment for the use of something you've created or own—represents one of the most leveraged income streams available. Unlike most other income sources, royalties allow you to create something once and potentially get paid for it indefinitely.

Royalty Income Strategies

Consider these approaches to generating royalty income:

1. **Book publishing:** Writing and publishing books, especially in digital formats with minimal production costs, can create ongoing royalty streams. Self-publishing platforms like Amazon KDP have democratized this opportunity.
2. **Music creation:** Composing, performing, and recording music generates royalties whenever the work is streamed, purchased, or used in media. Digital distribution platforms like DistroKid make this accessible to independent artists.

3. **Course creation:** Developing online courses on platforms like Udemy, Teachable, or Skillshare provides royalty-like income from student enrollments without requiring your ongoing time.
4. **Software and app development:** Creating useful software tools, whether mobile apps or specialized programs, can generate ongoing revenue through purchases, subscriptions, or licensing.
5. **Photography and stock media:** Creating and licensing visual content through stock photography and video platforms provides passive income when others use your work.
6. **Patents and inventions:** Developing innovative solutions to problems and securing intellectual property protection allows you to license your inventions to manufacturers.
7. **Brand development and licensing:** Creating recognizable brands that can be licensed to manufacturers adds a revenue stream without production responsibilities.

For Black creators in particular, royalty income offers a powerful opportunity to capitalize on our cultural contributions while retaining ownership and control—something historically denied to many Black artists, inventors, and creators.

The Creator Ecosystem Strategy

To maximize royalty potential, consider implementing a creator ecosystem strategy:

1. Develop expertise and audience in a specific niche
2. Create multiple complementary products in various formats (books, courses, downloadable tools, membership communities)

3. Build systems to market these products with minimal ongoing effort
4. Continuously reinvest a portion of your royalty income into creating new intellectual property
5. Leverage each new creation to promote your existing product ecosystem

This approach creates synergy between your various intellectual properties, with each one helping to sell the others while serving your audience at different price points and through different learning modalities.

Tanya, a former elementary school teacher we advised, implemented this strategy by creating educational materials based on her classroom experience. She began with printable activities on Teachers Pay Teachers, expanded to digital courses for fellow educators, and eventually published books on effective teaching methods. Her creator ecosystem now generates more income than her former teaching salary while reaching educators worldwide.

CHAPTER 2: BROADEN YOUR EARNINGS

Strategically Combining Income Streams

The true power of multiple income streams emerges when they're strategically combined rather than developed in isolation. Consider these principles for effective income stream integration:

1. Start with Complementary Streams

Look for income opportunities that leverage the same skills, resources, or relationships but in different ways. For example:

- A real estate agent might generate commission income (earned), property management fees (business), and rental income (real estate)
- A graphic designer might earn freelance income (earned), sell digital templates (royalties), and invest in design-focused companies (dividends)
- A healthcare professional might work traditional shifts (earned), consult for healthcare companies (business), and invest in healthcare REITs (dividends and capital gains)

This approach maximizes return on your knowledge, network, and effort while creating natural synergies between your income sources.

2. Balance Active and Passive Streams

Some income streams require your time and active participation, while others generate revenue with minimal ongoing involvement. A resilient income portfolio includes both types:

Active streams (requiring your time):

- Earned income from employment
- Service-based businesses
- Active trading or real estate management

Passive streams (requiring little/no time after setup):

- Dividend and interest income
- Established rental properties with management
- Royalties from created content
- Automated online businesses

While passive income is often idealized, active income typically provides higher returns on time invested, especially initially. The optimal approach usually involves using active income to build assets that eventually generate passive income.

3. Consider Tax Efficiency

Different income streams receive different tax treatment. Strategic planning can significantly impact your after-tax income:

- Earned income faces the highest tax rates and self-employment taxes

- Qualified dividends and long-term capital gains receive preferential tax rates
- Rental income benefits from depreciation deductions
- Business income offers numerous tax advantages and deductions
- Roth IRA withdrawals in retirement are completely tax-free

Working with a tax professional to optimize the structure and timing of your various income streams can substantially increase your effective income without changing the underlying activities.

4. Create Funding Pipelines

Design your income streams to automatically fund each other's growth:

- Use earned income to invest in dividend-paying stocks
- Direct dividend income to purchase rental properties
- Allocate rental income to develop intellectual property
- Dedicate royalty income to acquire businesses

This systematic approach accelerates wealth building by continually converting active income into assets that generate passive income, which then creates more assets in a virtuous cycle.

Implementing Your Multiple Streams Strategy

With an understanding of the seven streams and their integration principles, let's develop a practical implementation plan:

Phase 1: Foundation Building (Months 1-6)

1. **Maximize your primary income source**
   - ☐ Negotiate your current compensation if employed
   - ☐ Optimize your pricing and client acquisition if self-employed
   - ☐ Develop in-demand skills to increase your marketability
2. **Establish your first supplementary stream**
   - ☐ Choose based on your existing skills, interests, and resources
   - ☐ Start small with minimal investment or risk
   - ☐ Focus on validating the concept and generating initial revenue
3. **Begin regular investing for future passive income**
   - ☐ Set up automatic contributions to investment accounts
   - ☐ Focus initially on growth investments that will later provide dividends or capital gains
   - ☐ Start building investment knowledge alongside your portfolio

Phase 2: Expansion (Months 7-18)

1. **Scale your supplementary stream**
   - ☐ Increase marketing, capacity, or product offerings
   - ☐ Develop systems to make operations more efficient
   - ☐ Consider hiring help if appropriate
2. **Add a third income stream**
   - ☐ Choose one complementary to your existing streams
   - ☐ Apply lessons learned from your first supplementary stream
   - ☐ Leverage relationships and resources you've already developed
3. **Begin building passive income bases**
   - ☐ Expand investment portfolio with dividend focus
   - ☐ Consider entry-level real estate opportunities
   - ☐ Explore royalty potential in your area of expertise

Phase 3: Optimization (Months 19-36)

1. **Systematize existing streams**
   - ☐ Document processes for consistency and efficiency
   - ☐ Delegate or automate where possible
   - ☐ Eliminate underperforming activities
2. **Strategically add remaining streams**
   - ☐ Fill gaps in your income portfolio
   - ☐ Focus on diversification and risk management
   - ☐ Balance active and passive opportunities
3. **Integrate tax planning**
   - ☐ Structure activities for optimal tax treatment

- ☐ Time income and deductions strategically
- ☐ Utilize appropriate business entities

Phase 4: Acceleration (Ongoing)

1. **Reinvest for compound growth**
   - ☐ Direct profits from each stream toward expanding others
   - ☐ Focus on increasing passive income percentage over time
   - ☐ Build assets that appreciate while providing income
2. **Leverage success for new opportunities**
   - ☐ Use proven success to access bigger deals
   - ☐ Partner with others to expand capacity
   - ☐ Consider vertical integration within your strongest areas
3. **Create income stream redundancy**
   - ☐ Develop multiple sources within each major category
   - ☐ Reduce dependency on any single client, tenant, or platform
   - ☐ Prepare contingency plans for potential disruptions

Marcus: Five Years Later

Let's return to Marcus's story and see how implementing multiple income streams transformed his financial reality.

CHAPTER 2: BROADEN YOUR EARNINGS

After his corporate layoff, Marcus took several strategic actions:

1. He used his severance to purchase a small digital marketing agency from a retiring owner, providing immediate business income.
2. He accepted a position with a smaller company at 80% of his previous salary but with greater stability and a partial remote work arrangement, maintaining his earned income stream.
3. He invested 30% of his monthly savings in dividend-focused ETFs and 20% in growth ETFs for future capital gains.
4. He partnered with a former colleague to purchase a duplex, living in one unit and renting the other to offset his housing costs.
5. He created an online course teaching corporate professionals how to transition to agency ownership, generating royalty income.

Five years later, Marcus's financial picture has been transformed:

- His agency generates $180,000 annually in profit beyond his personal compensation
- He still maintains his corporate position, now earning $140,000
- His dividend portfolio provides $12,000 annually
- He owns three rental properties generating $30,000 in annual cash flow
- His online course and related digital products produce $45,000 yearly
- He strategically harvests capital gains of approximately $20,000 annually

From depending entirely on a single corporate paycheck, Marcus now enjoys over $425,000 in annual income from seven distinct streams. More importantly, only about 33% of his income requires his active daily participation. The rest would continue flowing even if he stepped back from active work.

"The layoff was the best thing that ever happened to me financially," Marcus reflected. "It forced me to stop thinking like an employee and start thinking like a business owner and investor. Now I have options I never imagined possible."

Your Journey to Multiple Income Streams

As we conclude this chapter, remember that developing multiple income streams is a journey, not an overnight transformation. Start where you are with the resources you have. Focus on one new stream at a time, building it to stability before adding another. Be patient with the process while remaining consistent in your actions.

The path to multiple income streams isn't about working seven different jobs or exhausting yourself with endless hustle. It's about strategically directing your time, knowledge, and resources toward building systems and assets that work for you. It's about transitioning from merely trading hours for dollars to creating sustained value that generates ongoing returns.

For Black families building generational wealth, multiple income streams provide not just financial benefits but freedom—freedom from dependency on any single employer, client, or market condition;

freedom to make choices based on your values rather than economic necessity; freedom to build wealth on your own terms.

In the next chapter, we'll explore how to protect your growing income and assets through a robust financial freedom fund. But first, complete the action steps below to begin expanding your income streams.

ACTION STEP: Identify and Plan for at Least One New Income Stream

- [ ] **Inventory your assets**
  - [ ] Skills and expertise you've developed
  - [ ] Knowledge you possess that others value
  - [ ] Resources you already own (property, equipment, savings)
  - [ ] Relationships and networks you've built
- [ ] **Identify your first additional stream**
  - [ ] List 3-5 potential income opportunities that leverage your existing assets
  - [ ] Evaluate each based on startup requirements, income potential, and alignment with your interests
  - [ ] Select one to pursue first
- [ ] **Create an implementation plan**
  - [ ] Research your chosen opportunity thoroughly
  - [ ] Identify specific first steps to generate revenue
  - [ ] Set SMART goals with clear timelines
  - [ ] Allocate specific time and resources to this project

- ☐ **Design your long-term streams strategy**
    - ☐ Map out which of the seven streams you intend to develop
    - ☐ Create a tentative timeline for adding each stream
    - ☐ Identify how your streams will complement each other
    - ☐ Establish metrics to evaluate progress
- ☐ **Take immediate action**
    - ☐ Complete at least one concrete step toward your new income stream within 48 hours
    - ☐ Schedule regular time blocks dedicated to developing this stream
    - ☐ Identify an accountability partner or community for support

Remember: The goal isn't to create seven streams immediately, but to consistently move toward income diversification through strategic action.

CHAPTER 3

UNDERWRITE YOUR FINANCIAL FREEDOM FUND

"The time to repair the roof is when the sun is shining."
—John F. Kennedy

"We were living the dream until we weren't," Patricia told us, her voice steady but her eyes revealing the trauma of the past year.

Patricia and her husband Robert had built what seemed like the perfect life. Both healthcare professionals—she a nurse practitioner, he a physical therapist—they earned a combined income of over $220,000. They had purchased their dream home in a desirable suburb, drove luxury vehicles, took memorable family vacations, and provided their two children with every opportunity, from private school to elite sports programs.

Then came the pandemic of 2020. The healthcare facility where Robert worked shut down its outpatient rehabilitation services. Three weeks later, the elective surgery center where Tanya was employed followed suit. Their steady income evaporated virtually overnight.

"We had less than $5,000 in savings," Robert admitted. "We'd always relied on our next paycheck. With our income, we never thought we needed to worry about saving for emergencies."

Within two months, they had maxed out their credit cards. By month four, they were behind on their mortgage. By month six, their cars had been repossessed. The financial stress took a toll on their marriage, their health, and their children's sense of security.

"The hardest part wasn't even the financial hardship," Patricia reflected. "It was the realization that we'd been living in a financial fantasy. All that education, all that income—and we were just one crisis away from disaster."

Patricia and Robert's story illustrates a painful truth that many successful Black professionals discover too late: Income alone doesn't create security. Without adequate savings, even high earners remain vulnerable to economic shocks, whether personal (job loss, illness, family emergency) or societal (recessions, pandemics, industry disruptions).

This vulnerability is why "Underwrite Your Financial Freedom Fund" is the third step in our Abundance Formula—and perhaps the most crucial foundation for your family's financial resilience.

Beyond the Emergency Fund: The Freedom Fund Mindset

Most financial advice includes building an "emergency fund" with 3-6 months of living expenses. This conventional wisdom is sound, but limited. The concept of a "Financial Freedom Fund" represents a more empowered approach with three key distinctions:

1. **Perspective shift:** An "emergency fund" focuses on crisis and scarcity. A "Freedom Fund" emphasizes opportunity and agency. This shift transforms saving from a defensive action to an empowering one.
2. **Expanded purpose:** While emergency funds are reserved for unexpected negative events, Freedom Funds serve multiple functions—providing security during hardship, yes, but also creating options, enabling strategic career or business moves, and funding valuable opportunities.
3. **Targeted size:** Traditional emergency funds are sized based on conventional wisdom rather than individual circumstances. A properly structured Freedom Fund is calculated based on your specific situation, risk profile, and goals.

For Black families building wealth, this reframing is particularly important. Our historical relationship with financial systems has often been marked by exclusion, discrimination, and exploitation. A robust Freedom Fund represents not just financial prudence but a form of self-determination and empowerment.

Calculating Your Freedom Fund Number

The first step in underwriting your Financial Freedom Fund is determining how much you need. While the standard advice of 3-6 months of expenses provides a starting point, a truly adequate fund requires more nuanced calculation.

Factors Affecting Your Freedom Fund Size

Consider these variables when determining your optimal Freedom Fund size:

1. **Income stability:** Those with variable or commission-based income need larger funds than those with stable, predictable paychecks.
2. **Income sources:** Families with multiple income streams have lower risk than single-income households and may require smaller cushions.
3. **Industry volatility:** Workers in fields prone to layoffs, seasonal fluctuations, or technological disruption need larger reserves than those in stable sectors.
4. **Specialized skills:** Those with highly specialized skills that limit alternative employment options need greater reserves than those with transferable skills.
5. **Health status:** Families with ongoing medical needs or conditions should maintain larger funds to cover potential health-related costs.
6. **Family structure:** Single parents or sole breadwinners require larger safety nets than dual-income households where risk is distributed.
7. **Network strength:** Those with robust professional networks that could facilitate quick reemployment may need smaller funds than those with limited connections.
8. **Location:** Residents of areas with diverse employment opportunities may need smaller reserves than those in regions dependent on a single industry.

CHAPTER 3: UNDERWRITE YOUR FINANCIAL FREEDOM FUND

The Freedom Fund Formula

To calculate your baseline Freedom Fund target:

1. **Determine your essential monthly expenses:**
   - Housing (mortgage/rent, property taxes, insurance)
   - Utilities (electricity, gas, water, internet, phone)
   - Food (groceries, not dining out)
   - Transportation (car payment, insurance, gas, maintenance or public transit)
   - Healthcare (insurance premiums, regular medications)
   - Childcare (if applicable)
   - Minimum debt payments
   - Other unavoidable expenses
2. **Multiply by your risk factor:**

   - Minimum: 6 months (for dual-income households in stable industries with strong networks)
   - Standard: 8 months (for most situations)
   - Enhanced: 12 months (for single-income households, volatile industries, specialized skills, or health concerns)
   - Maximum: 18+ months (for entrepreneurs, commission-based earners, or those with multiple risk factors)

For Patricia and Robert, their essential monthly expenses totaled approximately $10,000. Given their specialized healthcare roles and the unpredictable nature of healthcare industry restructuring, they needed at least a 12-month fund—meaning a Freedom Fund target of $120,000.

"That number felt impossible when we first calculated it," Patricia admitted. "But once we broke it down into smaller goals, it became our top financial priority."

The Progressive Freedom Fund Approach

Building a substantial Freedom Fund doesn't happen overnight, especially when starting from zero. The Progressive Freedom Fund approach breaks this substantial goal into manageable stages, each providing increasing levels of security and freedom.

Stage 1: Mini Emergency Fund ($1,000-$2,500)

This initial fund covers minor emergencies like car repairs, unexpected medical expenses, or appliance replacements. Even this modest amount prevents countless small emergencies from escalating into financial crises by eliminating the need for high-interest debt.

Timeline goal: 1-3 months

Strategies for rapid accumulation:

- Temporarily reduce all non-essential spending
- Sell unused or unnecessary possessions
- Take on short-term overtime or gig work
- Redirect windfalls like tax refunds or gifts
- Temporarily pause retirement contributions beyond employer match

Stage 2: Basic Security Fund (1 month of expenses)

This milestone provides breathing room for job transitions, temporary income reductions, or more significant emergencies. It represents your first full month of financial independence from the paycheck-to-paycheck cycle.

Timeline goal: 3-6 months

Accumulation strategies:

- Implement aggressive but sustainable budget cuts
- Evaluate and eliminate or reduce regular subscriptions
- Negotiate bills (insurance, phone, internet, etc.)
- Automate weekly or bi-weekly transfers to savings
- Continue directing windfalls to this fund

Stage 3: Intermediate Freedom Fund (3 months of expenses)

At this stage, you gain significant financial resilience. Three months of expenses provides cushion for most common financial disruptions, from job loss to medical issues to major home repairs.

Timeline goal: 6-12 months

Accumulation strategies:

- Maintain moderate budget optimization
- Consider a side hustle dedicated to building this fund

- Evaluate ways to reduce major expenses (housing, transportation)
- Automate 5-10% of income toward this goal
- Begin developing additional income streams

Stage 4: Full Freedom Fund (6-12+ months of expenses)

Your complete Freedom Fund provides not just security but true financial freedom—the ability to make life and career decisions based on values rather than desperate necessity.

Timeline goal: 12-36 months

Accumulation strategies:

- Maintain automated contributions
- Direct raises and bonuses to this fund
- Allocate income from additional streams
- Consider strategic debt reduction alongside fund building
- Implement tax optimization strategies to increase available funds

For Robert and Patricia, implementing this progressive approach transformed their financial situation. Within 3 months, they had built their mini emergency fund of $2,000. Within 8 months, they had accumulated one full month of expenses. Two years later, they had their complete 12-month Freedom Fund—and a completely different relationship with money.

"Having that fund changed everything," Robert explained. "Not just our financial situation, but our stress levels, our marriage, our parenting. When you know you're financially secure, you show up differently in every area of life."

Where to Keep Your Freedom Fund

Building your fund is just the beginning—where and how you maintain it matters significantly. Your Freedom Fund needs to balance several sometimes-competing objectives:

- **Safety:** Principal must be protected from loss
- **Liquidity:** Funds should be readily accessible when needed
- **Growth:** Money should at least keep pace with inflation
- **Simplicity:** Management should require minimal time and expertise
- **Psychological separation:** Funds should be accessible but not too easily spent

Given these parameters, consider these options for housing your Freedom Fund:

High-Yield Savings Accounts (HYSAs)

Best for: Mini Emergency Fund and portions of larger funds needing immediate accessibility

Advantages:

- FDIC insured up to $250,000

- Complete liquidity with no penalties
- Higher interest rates than traditional savings
- Easy to set up and manage
- No market risk

Disadvantages:

- Interest rates typically below inflation
- May tempt spending if connected to regular accounts
- Funds accessible within 1-3 business days (not instant)

Implementation tip: Choose an online bank offering competitive rates without fees or minimum balances. Set up automatic transfers from your checking account on payday.

Money Market Accounts

Best for: Intermediate portions of your Freedom Fund

Advantages:

- FDIC insured up to $250,000
- Slightly higher interest than standard savings
- Limited check-writing or debit card access
- Maintained at traditional banks for easy access

Disadvantages:

- May have higher minimum balance requirements
- Limited transactions per month

- Still typically pays below inflation

Implementation tip: Compare rates across multiple institutions, including credit unions, which often offer better rates than traditional banks.

Certificates of Deposit (CDs)

Best for: Portions of larger Freedom Funds not needed immediately

Advantages:

- FDIC insured up to $250,000
- Higher interest rates than savings accounts
- Fixed terms prevent impulsive spending
- Predictable returns

Disadvantages:

- Early withdrawal penalties
- Locked interest rates (disadvantage in rising rate environments)
- Minimum deposit requirements

Implementation tip: Consider a CD ladder with staggered maturity dates to provide regular access to portions of your funds while maintaining higher interest rates.

Treasury Bills and Notes

Best for: Larger Freedom Funds seeking government-backed security

Advantages:

- Backed by full faith and credit of U.S. government
- Exempt from state and local taxes
- Various maturity options (4 weeks to 10 years)
- Typically higher yields than savings accounts
- Can be purchased directly from Treasury

Disadvantages:

- Less liquid than savings accounts
- Potential penalties for early redemption
- Slightly more complex to purchase and manage

Implementation tip: Consider Treasury bills for portions of your fund with 3-12 month time horizons. Purchase through TreasuryDirect.gov to avoid broker fees.

I Bonds

Best for: Longer-term portions of larger Freedom Funds seeking inflation protection

Advantages:

- Backed by U.S. government
- Interest rate combines fixed rate plus inflation adjustment
- Exempt from state and local taxes
- Excellent inflation protection

- No market risk

Disadvantages:

- $10,000 purchase limit per person per year
- Cannot be redeemed in first 12 months
- Three-month interest penalty if redeemed before 5 years
- Must be purchased through TreasuryDirect.gov

Implementation tip: Consider allocating a portion of your Freedom Fund to I Bonds annually to build inflation protection over time, particularly in high-inflation environments.

Money Market Mutual Funds

Best for: Larger Freedom Funds seeking slightly higher yields with minimal additional risk

Advantages:

- Typically higher yields than bank accounts
- Daily liquidity with no penalties
- Low expense ratios
- Can be linked to brokerage accounts for easy transfers

Disadvantages:

- Not FDIC insured (though historically very safe)
- May have minimum investment requirements
- Yield fluctuates with market conditions

Implementation tip: Choose funds with the lowest expense ratios from established providers like Vanguard, Fidelity, or Schwab.

The Hybrid Approach

Rather than choosing a single vehicle for your entire Freedom Fund, consider a hybrid approach that balances accessibility, yield, and psychological barriers:

Tier 1: Immediate Access (20-30% of total fund)

- High-yield savings account
- Accessible within 1-3 business days
- For immediate emergencies and opportunities

Tier 2: Short-Term Access (30-40% of total fund)

- Money market funds or short-term CDs
- Accessible within 1-2 weeks
- For expected needs within 3-6 months

Tier 3: Extended Access (30-50% of total fund)

- Longer-term CDs, I Bonds, or Treasury notes
- Accessible with some planning
- For less likely scenarios or longer-term disruptions

This tiered approach maximizes yield while ensuring appropriate liquidity and creating psychological barriers that prevent casual access for non-emergency purposes.

For Patricia and Robert, the hybrid approach meant keeping $30,000 (25% of their fund) in a high-yield savings account, $40,000 (33%) in a ladder of 3-6 month CDs, and $50,000 (42%) in I Bonds purchased gradually over several years. This structure gave them both security and yield while protecting their fund from impulsive access.

Building Your Freedom Fund Systematically

While the size of your target Freedom Fund might seem daunting initially, systematic approaches can transform it from an intimidating goal to an achievable reality.

Automation: The Foundation of Success

The most effective Freedom Fund building strategy removes human decision-making from the equation. Automation leverages behavioral psychology by making saving the default rather than requiring repeated conscious choices.

Implementation strategies:

1. Set up direct deposit to automatically divert a percentage of your paycheck to your Freedom Fund accounts
2. Establish automatic transfers that occur immediately after payday
3. Use apps like Digit or Qapital that analyze spending patterns and automatically save "safe" amounts
4. Implement employer split-deposits if available
5. Automate escalation by scheduling periodic increases to your contribution percentage

For most people, money that never appears in their checking account is money they won't miss. Automation leverages this psychological reality.

Accelerated Growth Strategies

Beyond regular contributions, these strategies can significantly accelerate your Freedom Fund growth:

1. **Income windfalls:** Direct 90-100% of tax refunds, bonuses, gifts, inheritance, settlements, or other unexpected income to your Freedom Fund until fully funded.
2. **Expense elimination:** Conduct a "financial fast" by dramatically reducing discretionary spending for a defined period (30-90 days) and redirecting all savings to your fund.
3. **Spending audits:** Systematically review recurring expenses and subscriptions monthly, eliminating those providing minimal value. Channel the savings to your fund.
4. **Income boosting:** Dedicate income from overtime, side hustles, or temporary second jobs specifically to your Freedom Fund. Knowing this work directly builds your security provides additional motivation.
5. **Resource conversion:** Convert underutilized assets (unused vehicles, recreational equipment, collections, etc.) into Freedom Fund contributions through sales.
6. **Debt-to-savings pivot:** Once high-interest debts are eliminated, redirect those previous payment amounts to your Freedom Fund, maintaining the same total outflow.
7. **Financial windfalls:** Leverage special programs like the Earned Income Tax Credit, child tax credits, stimulus payments, or educational grants to boost your fund.

8. **Incremental improvement:** Increase your savings rate by 1% every 60-90 days. This gradual approach creates minimal lifestyle impact while substantially accelerating progress.

Behavioral Success Strategies

Building a substantial Freedom Fund isn't just about financial mechanics—it's also about psychology. These behavioral strategies support consistent progress:

1. **Visual tracking:** Create visible representations of your progress—thermometer charts, visual trackers, or apps that gamify saving. Seeing progress builds motivation.
2. **Milestone celebrations:** Establish meaningful rewards for reaching key milestones. Celebrations reinforce the behavior while providing positive association.
3. **Accountability partnerships:** Share your goals with trusted friends or family who will check in on your progress and provide encouragement.
4. **Purpose connection:** Regularly visualize specific scenarios where your Freedom Fund would protect your family. This emotional connection strengthens resolve during temptation.
5. **Identity reframing:** Begin thinking of yourself as a "saver" or "wealth builder" rather than a "spender." This identity shift naturally aligns actions with your financial goals.
6. **Progress journaling:** Document your journey, including challenges overcome and benefits realized. This record provides motivation during difficult periods.

7. **Community engagement:** Join communities (online or in-person) of others building similar financial foundations. Shared experiences provide both practical strategies and emotional support.
8. **Future-self connection:** Write letters to your future self describing how building this fund will transform your opportunities and security. Read these during moments of financial temptation.

For Robert and Patricia, automation formed the foundation of their Freedom Fund strategy. They set up separate direct deposits, with 15% of their reinstated incomes going directly to their fund accounts. They accelerated this foundation with strategic choices: living in a modest apartment while rebuilding, directing all overtime pay to their fund, and selling luxury items they had previously accumulated.

"The behavioral strategies were just as important as the financial ones," Patricia noted. "Creating vision boards with our kids about what financial security would mean for our family made it a shared mission rather than a deprivation."

Protecting Your Freedom Fund

Building your fund requires discipline and sacrifice. Protecting it requires boundaries—both financial and psychological.

CHAPTER 3: UNDERWRITE YOUR FINANCIAL FREEDOM FUND

Creating Meaningful Access Barriers

To prevent casual raiding of your Freedom Fund, establish clear barriers that require conscious decisions:

1. **Separate institutions:** Maintain your Freedom Fund at different financial institutions than your day-to-day accounts, eliminating the temptation of easy transfers.
2. **Account segmentation:** Create separate accounts for different purposes rather than commingling all funds. This clarifies the specific purpose of each account.
3. **Two-person authorization:** For couples, consider requiring both partners to approve significant withdrawals, creating a built-in review process.
4. **Cooling-off periods:** Implement personal rules requiring 24-72 hours between deciding to access funds and actually making the withdrawal.
5. **Physical barriers:** For portions of smaller funds, consider less convenient access methods, such as savings bonds or accounts without debit card access.
6. **Documentation requirements:** Create a personal system requiring written justification for any Freedom Fund withdrawal, forcing conscious reflection.
7. **Replacement commitments:** Before withdrawing, establish concrete plans for replenishing any funds used, maintaining accountability to your goals.

Defining Appropriate Use Cases

To maintain the integrity of your Freedom Fund, clearly define what constitutes legitimate use versus inappropriate access:

Appropriate uses may include:

- Job loss or significant income reduction
- Essential medical expenses not covered by insurance
- Critical home or vehicle repairs
- Unexpected tax obligations
- Essential family emergency travel
- Covering essential expenses during disability before benefits begin
- Funding essential education or certification for career transition
- Capital for entrepreneurial opportunities with high probability of success

Inappropriate uses typically include:

- Lifestyle enhancements or luxury purchases
- Discretionary travel or entertainment
- Down payments for homes or vehicles beyond your means
- Holiday or gift spending
- Regular budgeting shortfalls
- Investing in volatile assets or speculative opportunities
- Lending to friends or family
- Business ventures without thorough planning

Creating clear guidelines in advance—ideally in writing—provides an objective standard when emotional situations arise.

CHAPTER 3: UNDERWRITE YOUR FINANCIAL FREEDOM FUND

Maintaining Discipline During Temptation

Even with barriers and guidelines, moments of temptation will inevitably arise. These strategies help maintain discipline:

1. **Question framework:** When tempted, ask: "Is this a true emergency or opportunity, or merely a desire? What alternatives exist? How would I feel about this decision in 6 months?"
2. **Advisor consultation:** Identify a financially prudent friend, family member, or professional who can provide objective perspective during temptation.
3. **Alternative sourcing:** Before accessing your Freedom Fund, systematically explore all other options—budget adjustments, payment plans, negotiation, temporary income increases, or minimal credit use.
4. **Partial solutions:** If access is truly necessary, withdraw the minimum required rather than convenient rounded amounts, preserving as much of your fund as possible.
5. **Future impact assessment:** Calculate the true cost of withdrawals by estimating the future value of those funds if left to compound, creating awareness of the real sacrifice.

For Patricia and Robert, protecting their rebuilt Freedom Fund became a sacred commitment. They maintained accounts at a separate credit union from their checking accounts and implemented a "72-hour rule" for any potential withdrawals.

"We've had moments of temptation," Robert acknowledged. "When we wanted to upgrade our cars or take an expensive vacation. But we always come back to remembering what it felt like to have nothing between us and financial disaster. That memory is powerful."

Using Your Freedom Fund Strategically

While protection is essential, remember that your Freedom Fund exists to be used when truly needed. When legitimate needs or opportunities arise, these principles guide optimal usage:

Emergency Response Strategies

When facing genuine financial emergencies:

1. **Maintain perspective:** Remember that using your fund for legitimate emergencies is not failure—it's precisely why you built it in the first place.
2. **Implement tiered access:** Begin with your most accessible funds, preserving longer-term or higher-yielding portions until necessary.
3. **Minimize withdrawal size:** Calculate the minimum required to address the immediate need rather than estimating or withdrawing rounded amounts.
4. **Create replenishment plans:** Immediately establish concrete strategies for rebuilding your fund, beginning with the next pay period.
5. **Evaluate prevention:** After addressing the emergency, analyze whether better planning, insurance, or systems could prevent similar future occurrences.

6. **Document learnings:** Record your experience, including what worked well and what you'd do differently, creating a personal playbook for future situations.

Opportunity Maximization Strategies

When evaluating potential opportunities:

1. **Apply rigorous analysis:** Assess risk, return potential, and opportunity cost thoroughly before using Freedom Fund resources.
2. **Calculate ROI timeline:** Determine how quickly the opportunity could replenish the funds used and what contingencies exist if projections aren't met.
3. **Consider partial funding:** Explore whether the opportunity could be pursued with partial funding from your Freedom Fund combined with other resources.
4. **Evaluate alternatives:** Explore whether the opportunity could be funded through other means—business loans, partner capital, or staged implementation.
5. **Implement success triggers:** Establish specific metrics that indicate when to continue investing in the opportunity versus when to preserve remaining funds.
6. **Maintain reserve ratios:** Consider preserving at least 50% of your original Freedom Fund even when pursuing opportunities, maintaining core security.

The Freedom Fund Maintenance System

Once you've built your fund, implement a sustainable maintenance system:

1. **Quarterly reviews:** Schedule regular evaluations of your fund's size, allocation, and yield optimization.
2. **Annual reassessments:** Review your overall financial situation yearly to determine whether your Freedom Fund target remains appropriate or needs adjustment.
3. **Inflation adjustments:** Increase your fund periodically to maintain purchasing power as your expenses and inflation rise.
4. **Yield optimization:** Research current rates across various vehicles at least twice yearly, moving funds strategically to maximize returns while maintaining safety and liquidity.
5. **Tax planning:** Coordinate with your overall tax strategy to minimize any tax implications from interest earned.
6. **Documentation updates:** Maintain current records of all account information, access procedures, and intended use guidelines, sharing with trusted family members.
7. **Integration with estate planning:** Ensure your Freedom Fund is properly addressed in your will and estate documents, with clear direction for surviving family members.
8. **Balance maintenance:** When your fund exceeds your target, intentionally redirect surplus to other wealth-building priorities rather than allowing indefinite growth.

Beyond Financial Security: The Psychological Impact

The benefits of a fully-funded Freedom Fund extend far beyond financial metrics. Our clients consistently report profound psychological and lifestyle transformations:

Liberation from Financial Anxiety

Financial stress has been linked to numerous health problems, from insomnia and headaches to high blood pressure and heart disease. For many Black families in particular, financial anxiety represents a constant background stress that impacts all aspects of life.

A robust Freedom Fund doesn't just provide theoretical security—it dramatically reduces this chronic stress. Knowing you can weather financial disruptions for 6-12 months creates a sense of safety that permeates daily life.

"I used to wake up at 3 AM worrying about money," Patricia shared. "That completely stopped once we had our fund fully built. I can't overstate how much that improved my mental health."

Enhanced Career Autonomy

Without adequate savings, employment decisions are often driven by desperation rather than strategy or fulfillment. This reality keeps many talented individuals trapped in toxic work environments, unfulfilling careers, or exploitative arrangements.

A Freedom Fund transforms this dynamic by creating genuine choice. It provides the ability to:

- Leave unfulfilling or abusive work environments
- Negotiate confidently for better compensation or conditions
- Take time between positions to find ideal opportunities
- Pursue additional education or certification
- Transition to more meaningful career paths
- Consider entrepreneurial opportunities

This autonomy doesn't just benefit individuals—it transforms family dynamics by modeling agency and self-determination for the next generation.

Improved Relationship Dynamics

Financial stress ranks among the leading causes of relationship conflict and divorce. By removing or reducing this stress factor, a Freedom Fund often transforms relationship dynamics:

- Reducing arguments about day-to-day financial decisions
- Creating space for focus on shared values and goals
- Minimizing power imbalances related to income differences
- Building mutual respect through shared achievement
- Providing foundation for deeper financial partnership

"Building our Freedom Fund together actually strengthened our marriage," Robert reflected. "Going through that process forced us to align our values and priorities in ways we never had before."

Generational Pattern Breaking

For many Black families, financial insecurity has been an intergenerational pattern—not from lack of effort or intelligence, but from systemic barriers to wealth accumulation and emergency resource access.

Creating a substantial Freedom Fund often represents a profound break from these patterns—a declaration that financial vulnerability stops with your generation. This act of empowerment ripples through family systems, changing not just your financial reality but your children's relationship with money.

When Patricia and Robert's children participated in building their family's new Freedom Fund—helping to sell unused items, celebrating milestones, participating in "financial health" family meetings—they absorbed powerful lessons about financial responsibility, delayed gratification, and strategic planning.

"Our kids now understand money differently than either of us did growing up," Patricia noted. "They know what security feels like. That's a gift neither of our parents could give us, and it changes everything about their financial future."

Patricia and Robert: Four Years Later

Let's check in on Patricia and Robert's progress four years after their financial awakening.

They've not only built their full 12-month Freedom Fund of $120,000 but have optimized its structure for both security and return:

- $30,000 in a high-yield savings account for immediate access
- $40,000 in a CD ladder with 3-6 month maturities
- $50,000 in I Bonds for inflation protection

More importantly, their relationship with money has fundamentally transformed:

- They live in a comfortable but modest home with a manageable mortgage
- They drive reliable vehicles without luxury car payments
- They've increased their income through strategic career moves
- They've built multiple income streams through healthcare consulting
- They save and invest over 30% of their income
- They've developed a wealth-building strategy beyond their Freedom Fund
- They sleep soundly at night, free from financial anxiety

"The pandemic and our financial collapse were painful," Robert reflected, "but they forced us to rebuild on a solid foundation. We're actually further ahead now than we would have been on our previous path."

Patricia added, "The Freedom Fund gave us something money can't buy—peace of mind. Now we're building wealth not from fear but from a place of security and possibility."

CHAPTER 3: UNDERWRITE YOUR FINANCIAL FREEDOM FUND

Your Freedom Fund Journey

As we conclude this chapter, remember that your Financial Freedom Fund isn't just about money—it's about creating options, security, and peace of mind for your family.

Whether you're starting from zero or already have some savings, approach this journey with patience and determination. Building adequate financial reserves takes time, but each dollar added strengthens your family's resilience and expands your options.

For Black families building generational wealth, a robust Freedom Fund represents more than personal financial security—it's an act of liberation from systems designed to keep us vulnerable and dependent. It creates space to build wealth on your own terms, make decisions based on values rather than desperation, and model financial empowerment for future generations.

In the next chapter, we'll explore how to nurture your creditworthiness and use credit strategically as a wealth-building tool. But first, complete the action steps below to begin building your Freedom Fund.

ACTION STEP: Calculate Your Financial Freedom Fund Goal and Set a Savings Plan

- [ ] **Calculate your essential monthly expenses**
    - [ ] Housing costs: $ _____
    - [ ] Utilities: $ _____
    - [ ] Food (groceries only): $ _____
    - [ ] Transportation (essential only): $ _____
    - [ ] Healthcare: $ _____
    - [ ] Childcare (if applicable): $ _____
    - [ ] Minimum debt payments: $ _____
    - [ ] Other unavoidable expenses: $ _____
    - [ ] TOTAL: $ _____
- [ ] **Determine your risk factor multiplier**
    - [ ] Assess your income stability, industry, specialization, health status, and family structure
    - [ ] Select the appropriate multiplier: 6, 8, 12, or 18+ months
    - [ ] MULTIPLIER: _____ months
- [ ] **Calculate your Freedom Fund target**
    - [ ] Multiply your monthly expenses by your risk factor
    - [ ] TARGET: $ _____
- [ ] **Assess your current position**
    - [ ] Total all existing emergency savings
    - [ ] CURRENT SAVINGS: $ _____

CHAPTER 3: UNDERWRITE YOUR FINANCIAL FREEDOM FUND

- ☐ Calculate the gap between current savings and target
- ☐ GAP: $ _____
- ☐ **Create your progressive funding plan**
  - ☐ Stage 1 (Mini Fund): $ _____ by date: _____
  - ☐ Stage 2 (1 Month): $ _____ by date: _____
  - ☐ Stage 3 (3 Months): $ _____ by date: _____
  - ☐ Stage 4 (Full Fund): $ _____ by date: _____
- ☐ **Establish your funding mechanism**
  - ☐ Monthly contribution amount: $ _____
  - ☐ Source(s) of funds: _____
  - ☐ Automation method: _____
  - ☐ Acceleration strategies: _____
- ☐ **Determine your fund structure**
  - ☐ Immediate access vehicle: _____ Amount: $ _____
  - ☐ Short-term access vehicle: _____ Amount: $ _____
  - ☐ Extended access vehicle: _____ Amount: $ _____
- ☐ **Schedule your first progress review**
  - ☐ Date: _____
  - ☐ Metrics to evaluate: _____

Remember: Your Freedom Fund is the foundation that makes all other wealth-building activities possible. Prioritize it accordingly.

CHAPTER 4

NURTURE CREDITWORTHINESS AND USE CREDIT TO BUILD WEALTH

"Neither a borrower nor a lender be—unless you understand how to use credit as a wealth-building tool."
— Modern adaptation of Shakespeare

Andre had always been proud of his approach to money. Unlike many of his peers who flashed designer clothes and luxury cars they couldn't afford, he lived within his means. He drove a used car he'd paid for in cash. He rented a modest apartment while saving for a down payment. He used his debit card for purchases and avoided credit cards entirely.

"I don't believe in debt," he told us during our first meeting. "My parents always said, 'if you can't afford to pay cash, you can't afford it.' I've lived by that rule my whole life."

Andre's discipline was admirable, but it had led to an unexpected problem. At 32, with a stable career as an IT specialist and substantial savings, he decided it was time to purchase his first home. That's when he discovered that despite his financial responsibility, he had no credit score at all.

"The mortgage broker looked at me like I was from another planet," Andre recalled. "He said my lack of credit history made me a higher risk than someone with mediocre credit. How does that make any sense?"

Andre's story highlights a crucial reality that many financially conservative individuals discover too late: in today's financial system, avoiding credit entirely can be just as limiting as misusing it. This reality is why "Nurture Creditworthiness and Use Credit to Build Wealth" is the fourth step in our Abundance Formula.

Beyond Good and Bad: Reframing Our Relationship with Credit

For many in the Black community, skepticism toward debt and credit runs deep—and with good reason. Historically, predatory lending practices have disproportionately targeted our communities. From redlining that denied mortgages in Black neighborhoods to higher interest rates for equivalent credit profiles, the system has often worked against us.

This history has created a protective response in many families: avoid debt at all costs. Parents and grandparents who experienced discrimination or witnessed its effects often instilled firm warnings against borrowing. "Pay cash," "Stay out of debt," and "Don't trust banks" became financial commandments passed down through generations.

CHAPTER 4: NURTURE CREDITWORTHINESS AND USE CREDIT TO BUILD WEALTH

While this caution protected many families from predatory practices, it also created unintended consequences. In today's financial system, credit isn't just about borrowing money—it's a tool that, when used strategically, can accelerate wealth building rather than hinder it.

The first step in nurturing your creditworthiness is reframing your relationship with credit:

1. **Credit as a tool, not a crutch:** Like any tool, credit can be used productively or destructively depending on how it's wielded. The goal isn't to avoid the tool but to master its use.
2. **Credit as access infrastructure:** In today's economy, good credit provides access to opportunities, from housing and employment to insurance rates and business capital.
3. **Credit as leverage:** When used strategically, credit allows you to control valuable assets with minimal capital, accelerating wealth building.
4. **Credit as a wealth-building strategy:** The wealthy often use strategic borrowing to preserve and enhance their assets rather than liquidating them.

This reframing doesn't mean abandoning caution or forgetting historical lessons. It means approaching credit with knowledge and strategy rather than fear or avoidance.

Understanding Credit Scores: The Gatekeeper to Financial Opportunity

Your credit score serves as a financial passport that determines which opportunities are available to you and at what cost. Understanding how this score works is the first step to using it advantageously.

The Anatomy of a Credit Score

While several scoring models exist, the FICO score remains the most widely used. This three-digit number (ranging from 300-850) is calculated based on five key factors:

1. **Payment History (35%):** Whether you've paid past credit accounts on time. This is the most heavily weighted factor.
2. **Amounts Owed (30%):** How much you owe and how much of your available credit you're using (credit utilization).
3. **Length of Credit History (15%):** How long your credit accounts have been established, including the age of your oldest and newest accounts and the average age of all accounts.
4. **Credit Mix (10%):** The variety of credit accounts you have, including revolving accounts (credit cards) and installment accounts (mortgages, auto loans).
5. **New Credit (10%):** How many new accounts you've opened recently and how many recent inquiries appear on your report.

The impact of these factors isn't static—it varies based on your overall credit profile. For someone with limited credit history, a single late payment may have a more significant negative impact than for someone with decades of perfect payment history.

Credit Score Ranges and Their Implications

Your credit score typically falls within one of these ranges, each with different implications:

- **Exceptional (800-850):** Access to the best rates and terms, premium credit cards, and virtually guaranteed approval for most credit products.
- **Very Good (740-799):** Access to very competitive rates, though not always the absolute best offers available.
- **Good (670-739):** Considered "prime" credit; qualified for most credit products at decent (though not optimal) rates.
- **Fair (580-669):** May face higher interest rates, lower credit limits, and might be declined for some premium products.
- **Poor (300-579):** Limited credit options, typically with high interest rates, secured credit requirements, and significant limitations.

For Black families building wealth, striving for credit scores in the "Very Good" to "Exceptional" ranges (740+) creates substantial financial advantages. The difference between a 670 and 770 credit score on a $300,000 30-year mortgage could mean paying over $50,000 more in interest over the loan term.

Credit Bureaus and Reports: The Foundation of Your Score

Your credit score is derived from information contained in your credit reports, which are compiled by three major credit bureaus: Equifax, Experian, and TransUnion. These reports contain detailed information about:

- **Credit accounts:** Open and closed accounts, payment history, balances, credit limits
- **Public records:** Bankruptcies, foreclosures, tax liens
- **Inquiries:** Recent applications for credit
- **Personal information:** Name, address, employment history

Importantly, these bureaus don't always have identical information. Lenders may report to one, two, or all three bureaus, creating discrepancies between your reports and resulting scores.

For Andre, his absence from these credit reporting systems was the problem. Despite his financial responsibility, his lack of credit accounts meant the bureaus had nothing to report—and thus no basis for generating a credit score.

CHAPTER 4: NURTURE CREDITWORTHINESS AND USE CREDIT TO BUILD WEALTH

Building Credit from Zero: The Foundation Strategy

Whether you're starting from no credit history like Andre or rebuilding after financial challenges, these strategies establish a solid credit foundation:

1. Secured Credit Cards

Secured cards require a cash deposit that typically becomes your credit limit, minimizing risk for the issuer while helping you build credit.

Strategy implementation:

- Choose a card that reports to all three major credit bureaus
- Look for no annual fee options (Capital One Secured and Discover it Secured are strong choices)
- Keep utilization below 30% of your limit
- Pay the balance in full every month
- After 6-12 months of responsible use, request conversion to an unsecured card

2. Credit Builder Loans

These specialized products, offered by some credit unions and online lenders, place your "loan" amount in a secured account while you make payments, building payment history without actual borrowing.

Strategy implementation:

- Select loans with terms of 12-24 months for optimal credit-building effect
- Ensure the lender reports to all three bureaus
- Choose affordable monthly payments
- Set up automatic payments to ensure perfect payment history

3. Become an Authorized User

Being added to someone else's established credit card account can transfer their positive history to your credit report.

Strategy implementation:

- Choose someone with excellent payment history and low utilization
- Ideally, select accounts that have been open for several years
- Confirm the issuer reports authorized user activity to credit bureaus
- You don't need to use the card to benefit from this strategy

4. Retail or Store Credit Cards

These cards are typically easier to qualify for than major credit cards, making them good starter options.

Strategy implementation:

- Select cards from retailers you already frequent
- Look for no annual fee options
- Pay balances in full each month to avoid high interest rates
- Use sparingly and strategically

5. Report Non-Credit Payments

Some services allow you to add recurring payments like rent, utilities, and streaming subscriptions to your credit report.

Strategy implementation:

- Explore services like Experian Boost, eCredable, or Rental Kharma
- Focus on payments with perfect history
- Verify which bureaus receive the information
- Understand the impact may vary by scoring model

For Andre, implementing these strategies quickly established his credit profile. He started with a secured credit card, became an authorized user on his mother's long-standing credit card, and used Experian Boost to add his utility payment history. Within six months, he had established a credit score of 675. Within a year, his score had risen to 720—sufficient to qualify for a conventional mortgage.

"I went from credit invisible to mortgage-ready in about 14 months," Andre shared. "I wish I had understood earlier that using credit responsibly isn't the same as being irresponsible with money."

Elevating to Excellent Credit: The 700+ Club Strategies

Once you've established a credit foundation, these strategies will help you reach and maintain excellent credit scores (700+):

1. Perfect Payment History

Nothing impacts your credit score more significantly than consistent on-time payments.

Strategy implementation:

- Set up automatic payments for at least the minimum due on all accounts
- Create calendar reminders several days before due dates
- Build a one-month financial buffer to ensure payments even during tight months
- Address potential late payments proactively by contacting creditors before the due date

2. Strategic Credit Utilization

Keeping your credit utilization ratio low significantly impacts your score, second only to payment history.

Strategy implementation:

- Aim to keep overall utilization below 30%, with 10% or less being ideal for maximum scores

- Request credit limit increases every 6-12 months
- Consider making multiple payments throughout the month to keep reported balances low
- Keep accounts open even when not actively using them to maintain available credit
- Time major purchases to occur after your statement closing date but before payment due date

3. Credit Age Optimization

The average age of your accounts significantly impacts your score, with older accounts boosting your creditworthiness.

Strategy implementation:

- Keep your oldest accounts active with occasional small purchases
- Avoid closing old accounts, especially your oldest one
- When adding new accounts, consider the temporary negative impact on your average account age
- If you must close accounts, close newer ones first

4. Strategic Credit Mix

Maintaining both revolving accounts (credit cards) and installment accounts (loans) demonstrates your ability to manage different types of credit.

Strategy implementation:

- Maintain 2-3 credit cards with different issuers
- Consider adding an installment loan like an auto loan or small personal loan if you don't have one
- If you don't need an actual loan, consider a credit-builder loan specifically for diversification

5. Controlled New Credit Applications

Each credit application typically causes a small temporary drop in your score, while many applications in a short time can suggest financial distress.

Strategy implementation:

- Limit new credit applications to one every 6 months when possible
- Research qualification requirements before applying to avoid unlikely applications
- When shopping for specific loans (mortgage, auto), complete all applications within a 14-30 day window so they count as a single inquiry
- Avoid applying for credit before important financing events like mortgage applications

6. Regular Credit Monitoring and Disputing Errors

Credit report errors are surprisingly common and can significantly impact your score.

Strategy implementation:

- Review your free annual reports from all three bureaus at annualcreditreport.com
- Consider a credit monitoring service or use free monitoring through credit card issuers
- Dispute inaccuracies promptly through each bureau's formal dispute process
- Follow up on disputes and escalate when necessary

7. Strategic Debt Management

While some debt can help your credit, excessive debt can harm both your score and financial health.

Strategy implementation:

- Focus debt repayment on revolving accounts (credit cards) first
- Consider the "debt snowball" (paying smallest balances first) or "debt avalanche" (highest interest first) methods
- Avoid closing accounts immediately after paying them off
- Request goodwill adjustments for isolated late payments on otherwise perfect accounts

By implementing these strategies systematically, most people can achieve and maintain credit scores above 740—opening the door to the most favorable financing terms and opportunities.

For Andre, focusing on these "700+ Club" strategies after establishing his initial credit profile allowed him to boost his score to 760 within two years. This improvement qualified him for the best mortgage rates available, saving him thousands over the life of his home loan.

The "Buy, Borrow, Die" Strategy: How the Wealthy Use Credit

Beyond basic credit building lies a sophisticated approach used by many wealthy individuals to preserve and build wealth: the "Buy, Borrow, Die" strategy. While this approach requires substantial assets to implement fully, understanding its principles can inform your wealth-building strategy at any level.

The Three Phases Explained

1. **Buy:** Acquire appreciating assets that generate income, increase in value, or ideally both. These might include stocks, real estate, businesses, or other investments.
2. **Borrow:** Instead of selling these assets when you need capital (which would trigger taxes and halt their growth), borrow against them at favorable rates. This allows the assets to continue appreciating while providing liquidity.
3. **Die:** When you pass away, your heirs receive the assets with a "stepped-up basis" to the market value at your death,

potentially eliminating capital gains taxes that would have been due had you sold during your lifetime.

This strategy leverages several key advantages:

- **Tax efficiency:** Borrowed money isn't taxable income, unlike proceeds from selling appreciated assets, which trigger capital gains taxes.
- **Continued appreciation:** Assets continue growing even while you access their value through loans.
- **Lower effective costs:** For wealthy individuals, the interest cost of borrowing is often lower than the tax cost of selling assets.
- **Estate planning benefits:** Properly structured, this approach can significantly reduce estate tax burdens.

Strategic Credit Implementation at Various Wealth Levels

While the full "Buy, Borrow, Die" strategy requires substantial assets, elements of this approach can be implemented at different wealth stages:

Beginning Wealth Stage:

- Focus on building credit to access favorable financing for appreciating assets like your primary residence
- Use 0% APR credit offers strategically for short-term needs while keeping investments growing
- Consider leveraging retirement accounts as collateral for loans in true emergencies (though with caution)

Intermediate Wealth Stage:

- Utilize home equity lines of credit (HELOCs) for investment opportunities or major expenses instead of liquidating investments
- Explore securities-backed lines of credit (SBLOCs) once your portfolio reaches sufficient size
- Implement strategic borrowing for major purchases, comparing interest costs against investment returns

Advanced Wealth Stage:

- Establish banking relationships that provide premium lending options against various asset classes
- Create a coordinated borrowing strategy that spans multiple asset types (real estate, securities, business interests, etc.)
- Integrate borrowing strategy with estate planning to maximize wealth transfer efficiency

For Maya, a physician we advised, implementing elements of this strategy transformed her approach to financing major expenditures. Rather than liquidating her investment portfolio to purchase a vacation property, she established a securities-backed line of credit at 3.5% interest while her investments continued generating an average 8% return. This decision preserved her investment growth while providing the needed capital—a simplified version of the "Borrow" phase that created significant financial advantage.

CHAPTER 4: NURTURE CREDITWORTHINESS AND USE CREDIT TO BUILD WEALTH

Strategic Credit Applications for Wealth Building

Beyond maintaining excellent credit scores, strategic credit use can directly accelerate wealth building in several key areas:

1. Real Estate Acquisition and Optimization

Real estate remains one of the most accessible wealth-building vehicles, and strategic credit use can dramatically enhance its effectiveness.

Implementation strategies:

- Leverage excellent credit to secure optimal mortgage terms, potentially saving hundreds of thousands over a lifetime of real estate investments
- Utilize delayed financing strategies to quickly recover capital from cash purchases for additional investments
- Implement the BRRRR method (Buy, Rehabilitate, Rent, Refinance, Repeat) to recycle capital while building a real estate portfolio
- Establish HELOCs on properties during strong equity markets to have capital ready for future opportunities
- Use credit strategically for property improvements that increase value disproportionately to their cost

2. Business Establishment and Expansion

Access to capital often determines which businesses survive and thrive, making strategic credit use essential for entrepreneurs.

Implementation strategies:

- Leverage personal credit to secure initial business funding before establishing business credit
- Strategically use 0% APR offers for short-term business needs to maintain cash flow
- Build business credit profiles separate from personal credit to create additional borrowing capacity
- Utilize equipment financing to preserve capital for growth-focused activities
- Implement a strategic debt hierarchy, prioritizing lower-cost capital sources

3. Investment Amplification

Properly structured credit can enhance investment returns through leverage while managing risk.

Implementation strategies:

- Consider margin loans for short-term investment opportunities when expected returns significantly exceed interest costs
- Establish securities-backed lines of credit as lower-cost alternatives to margin for longer-term needs

CHAPTER 4: NURTURE CREDITWORTHINESS AND USE CREDIT TO BUILD WEALTH

- Use strategic borrowing to maintain market positions during temporary downturns rather than selling at losses
- Implement "cash-out" refinancing on investment properties to acquire additional assets during buying opportunities
- Consider life insurance policy loans for their unique advantages in certain investment scenarios

4. Education and Skill Enhancement

Investment in education and skills often provides the highest return on investment, and strategic credit can make these investments possible.

Implementation strategies:

- Evaluate education financing based on ROI rather than avoiding education debt entirely
- Prioritize federal student loans before private options for their superior protections and flexibility
- Consider income-based repayment strategies for professional degrees with high income potential
- Leverage employer tuition benefits whenever possible to minimize necessary borrowing
- Refinance education debt when your credit strength improves post-graduation

5. Tax Optimization

Strategic borrowing can create significant tax advantages when properly implemented.

Implementation strategies:

- Understand that interest on loans used for investments is often tax-deductible, reducing the effective cost of borrowing
- Leverage home equity debt strategically when tax advantages apply
- Consider the tax implications of different borrowing strategies, particularly for business purposes
- Implement coordinated borrowing and tax planning with qualified advisors
- Understand how the "Buy, Borrow, Die" strategy creates tax advantages through timing and basis adjustments

Protecting and Repairing Your Credit

Even with the best intentions, credit challenges can arise from economic downturns, health crises, or other unexpected events. Knowing how to protect and repair your credit is essential for long-term financial resilience.

Proactive Credit Protection Strategies

1. **Establish monitoring systems:** Use both free and paid services to receive alerts about changes to your credit profile, identifying potential issues early.
2. **Implement fraud alerts and credit freezes:** Consider placing fraud alerts on your credit files if you suspect identity theft risk, or freezing your credit entirely when not actively seeking new credit.

3. **Create credit utilization buffers:** Maintain credit utilization well below maximum thresholds to accommodate unexpected expenses without score damage.
4. **Develop creditor communication protocols:** Establish relationships with key creditors before problems arise, and know their hardship programs and contact procedures.
5. **Implement strategic account management:** Periodically use all open accounts to prevent closure due to inactivity, maintaining your available credit and account age.

Credit Recovery Strategies

If your credit has been damaged, these strategies can accelerate recovery:

1. **Address accuracy first:** Review all three credit reports for errors and dispute inaccuracies immediately, focusing on negative items.
2. **Negotiate settlements with "pay for delete" terms:** When settling old debts, negotiate removal of negative items rather than just "settled" status when possible.
3. **Request goodwill adjustments:** For isolated late payments amid otherwise perfect history, request goodwill adjustments from creditors, particularly for long-standing relationships.
4. **Implement credit rebuilding tools:** Use secured cards, credit builder loans, and authorized user strategies simultaneously to rebuild positive history.
5. **Dilute negative history:** Focus on building numerous positive accounts to minimize the impact of past negative items through the "percentage of accounts" effect.

6. **Address collections strategically:** Prioritize newer collections first, as older items have less impact as they age and eventually fall off your report.
7. **Consider professional assistance selectively:** While many credit repair services make exaggerated claims, legitimate credit attorneys can sometimes resolve complex issues more effectively than individual efforts.

When Lisa, a marketing executive we advised, experienced credit damage following a divorce and temporary job loss, these strategies helped her rebuild from a score of 580 to 720 within 18 months. This recovery allowed her to refinance her mortgage at a significantly lower rate, saving her $450 monthly—funds she then directed toward rebuilding her retirement savings.

"The recovery wasn't instant," Lisa noted, "but each month my score improved as I implemented these strategies consistently. The financial impact of that credit recovery has been life-changing."

The Family Credit Strategy: Building Creditworthiness Across Generations

For Black families building generational wealth, credit strength should be developed across generations rather than individually. This approach creates substantial advantages while addressing historical barriers to credit access.

Starting Early: Building Credit for Young Adults

Rather than having young adults start from zero, implement these strategies:

1. **Authorized user additions:** Add responsible teenagers to well-established credit card accounts, allowing them to begin adult life with credit history.
2. **Secured credit foundations:** Help young adults establish their own secured credit cards when legally able, providing guidance on responsible use.
3. **Education before access:** Ensure young adults understand credit mechanics before independently accessing credit, preventing early mistakes with long-term consequences.
4. **Co-signed strategic loans:** Consider carefully selected co-signing opportunities that build credit without creating undue risk (small credit-builder loans rather than major financing).
5. **Documentation training:** Teach proper record-keeping for credit accounts, disputes, and communication with creditors from the beginning.

Family Credit Strengthening Systems

Implementing family-wide credit strategies creates substantial advantages:

1. **Regular family credit reviews:** Schedule quarterly family financial meetings that include credit report reviews for all adult members.

2. **Shared monitoring services:** Utilize family plans for credit monitoring services to ensure all family members benefit from protection.
3. **Intergenerational credit building:** When appropriate, leverage stronger family members' credit to help others build through authorized user status, co-signing, or other structured arrangements.
4. **Emergency credit plans:** Develop family-wide strategies for protecting credit during financial emergencies, including communication templates and prioritization frameworks.
5. **Knowledge transfer systems:** Create systems ensuring credit knowledge passes between generations, preventing repeated learning through costly mistakes.

For the Washington family we advised, implementing these intergenerational strategies transformed their family's relationship with credit. The parents, who had struggled with credit challenges early in their marriage, ensured their three children entered adulthood with established credit profiles and thorough understanding of credit mechanics.

When their youngest son wanted to start a business after college, his excellent credit history—built through authorized user status since age 16 and careful independent credit management from age 18—allowed him to secure startup financing at favorable terms. This access to capital at a critical moment might not have been possible without the family's intentional credit strategy.

"We wanted our children to have credit advantages we didn't have," Mr. Washington explained. "Teaching them to use credit as a wealth-building tool rather than a consumption tool has given them options we never had at their age."

CHAPTER 4: NURTURE CREDITWORTHINESS AND USE CREDIT TO BUILD WEALTH

Andre: Three Years Later

Let's revisit Andre's story and see how implementing these credit strategies transformed his financial options.

After discovering his "credit invisibility," Andre implemented a comprehensive credit building strategy:

1. He secured two secured credit cards, using them for small monthly purchases and paying them in full.
2. He became an authorized user on his mother's oldest credit card.
3. He took out a small credit-builder loan through his credit union.
4. He used Experian Boost to add his utility and subscription payment history.
5. He implemented monitoring through Credit Karma and his credit card issuer's free monitoring service.

Within 18 months, Andre had built a credit score of 760—considered "excellent" by most lenders. This transformation created numerous financial advantages:

- He qualified for a mortgage with a 3.2% interest rate (compared to the 4.5%+ he would have faced with lower credit), saving him approximately $89,000 over the life of his loan.
- He obtained a premium rewards credit card that provided travel benefits and 2% cash back on all purchases, generating over $1,200 annually in rewards from his regular spending.
- He qualified for lower insurance premiums, saving approximately $800 annually on auto and homeowners policies.

- He established a home equity line of credit at prime rate, creating accessible capital for future investment opportunities.
- When starting a consulting business, he qualified for a business credit card with a $25,000 limit, providing valuable cash flow flexibility.

"I still live by my parents' core principle of financial responsibility," Andre reflected. "But I've learned that credit itself isn't the problem—it's how you use it. When used strategically, it creates opportunities that would be unavailable otherwise."

Your Credit Mastery Journey

As we conclude this chapter, remember that creditworthiness isn't just about qualifying for loans—it's about creating options, access, and financial advantages that accelerate your wealth-building journey.

Whether you're starting from zero like Andre, rebuilding after challenges, or looking to optimize already-good credit, implementing these strategies consistently will transform your relationship with the credit system.

For Black families building generational wealth, mastering credit represents both practical financial advantage and a form of systemic activism. By understanding and excelling within a system that has historically excluded us, we create new possibilities for ourselves while establishing patterns of financial empowerment for future generations.

In the next chapter, we'll explore how to strategically manage and eliminate liabilities that hinder wealth building while leveraging good debt for asset acquisition and growth. But first, complete the action steps below to begin optimizing your creditworthiness.

ACTION STEP: Assess Your Creditworthiness and Develop a Plan to Use Credit Strategically

- ☐ **Evaluate your current credit position**
  - ☐ Obtain your FICO scores from all three bureaus
  - ☐ Review your full credit reports for accuracy
  - ☐ Identify your credit score range: Poor, Fair, Good, Very Good, or Exceptional
  - ☐ Note specific factors affecting your score
- ☐ **Create your credit building or optimization plan**
  - ☐ If below 670: Focus on foundational building strategies
  - ☐ If 670-739: Implement "700+ Club" strategies
  - ☐ If 740+: Focus on maintenance and strategic credit use
  - ☐ Identify specific actions for your situation
- ☐ **Establish your credit protection system**
  - ☐ Select and implement a credit monitoring solution
  - ☐ Schedule regular credit review dates
  - ☐ Document dispute procedures for each bureau
  - ☐ Create emergency credit protection plans
- ☐ **Identify strategic credit uses for wealth building**
  - ☐ List potential wealth-building applications for your situation
  - ☐ Research specific credit products aligned with these goals

- ☐ Calculate potential ROI for strategic credit use
- ☐ Develop implementation timeline
- ☐ **Design your family credit strategy**
    - ☐ Identify opportunities for intergenerational credit building
    - ☐ Create credit education plan for family members
    - ☐ Schedule family credit review sessions
    - ☐ Document credit knowledge for transmission to next generation

Remember: Your creditworthiness is a valuable financial asset that, when properly managed, creates opportunities far beyond the ability to borrow money. Approach it with the same strategic attention you would give to any other significant asset.

CHAPTER 5

DIMINISH LIABILITIES

"Not all debt is created equal. The rich know the difference between good debt and bad debt—they avoid one and leverage the other."
—Robert Kiyosaki

"I'm drowning in debt, but I'm too afraid to even look at the numbers."

These words came from Michael, a 42-year-old corporate manager who reached out to us after attending one of our wealth-building seminars. On paper, Michael appeared successful—he earned a six-figure income, lived in a nice suburban home, and drove a luxury SUV. But beneath this veneer of prosperity lay a troubling reality.

When we finally convinced Michael to compile his complete financial picture, the truth was sobering. Between his mortgage, auto loans, student debt, credit cards, and personal loans, he owed nearly $780,000. His monthly debt payments consumed over 60% of his take-home pay, leaving little room for saving or investing. Despite a strong income, Michael was effectively working primarily to pay his creditors, with minimal wealth accumulation to show for his efforts.

"I make good money, but I feel broke all the time," he admitted. "I'm on a financial treadmill—running hard but going nowhere."

Michael's situation illustrates a common obstacle on the path to building wealth: excessive liabilities that drain resources away from asset accumulation. This obstacle is why "Diminish Liabilities" is the fifth step in our Abundance Formula.

The Liability Truth: Not All Debt Is Created Equal

The conventional wisdom many of us heard growing up was simple: "Debt is bad. Avoid it at all costs." While well-intentioned, this advice fails to recognize an important nuance that wealthy individuals and families have understood for generations: there's a profound difference between debt that enriches you and debt that impoverishes you.

Good Debt vs. Bad Debt: The Critical Distinction

Understanding this distinction is essential for building wealth:

Good Debt:

- Finances appreciating assets or income-producing opportunities
- Typically offers tax advantages
- Often has lower interest rates
- Creates more value than it costs
- Helps build wealth over time

Bad Debt:

- Finances depreciating assets or consumption
- Rarely offers tax advantages
- Typically carries higher interest rates
- Costs more than the value it creates
- Diminishes wealth over time

Examples of good debt might include mortgages for investment properties, business loans for promising ventures, or student loans for high-ROI education. Bad debt includes credit card balances carried month-to-month, auto loans for luxury vehicles, or personal loans for vacations and consumer purchases.

For Black families building wealth, this distinction is particularly important. Given the historical wealth gap and systemic barriers to wealth accumulation, we cannot afford the wealth-draining effects of bad debt. Every dollar paid in interest on consumer debt is a dollar diverted from asset acquisition and wealth building.

As we analyzed Michael's situation, we categorized his debts accordingly:

Good Debt:

- Primary residence mortgage: $320,000 (building equity in an appreciating asset)
- Rental property mortgage: $180,000 (generating monthly income)
- Student loans: $45,000 (increased earning potential)

Bad Debt:

- Credit card balances: $32,000 (primarily dining, travel, and consumer purchases)
- Auto loans: $78,000 (two luxury vehicles, both depreciating rapidly)
- Personal loans: $65,000 (home renovations, vacations, and past debt consolidation)
- Boat loan: $60,000 (rapidly depreciating lifestyle asset)

This categorization provided clarity about which debts were helping build Michael's wealth and which were actively preventing it.

The Wealth Impact of Liability Reduction

The true cost of carrying bad debt extends far beyond the interest paid—it includes the opportunity cost of what that money could have accomplished if directed toward wealth building instead.

Calculating the True Cost of Bad Debt

To understand the full impact of bad debt on wealth building, we need to consider:

1. **Direct interest costs:** The actual interest dollars paid to creditors
2. **Opportunity cost:** The potential growth of those same dollars if invested instead

3. **Time cost:** The delay in wealth milestones caused by debt service requirements
4. **Psychological cost:** The stress and limited options that accompany significant debt obligations

For Michael, we calculated that his bad debt (totaling $235,000) was costing him approximately $28,000 annually in direct interest payments. But the true cost became apparent when we calculated the opportunity cost:

If Michael redirected that $28,000 annual interest toward investments earning a conservative 8% annual return, he would accumulate approximately $1.5 million over 20 years. That's the real cost of his bad debt—not just the interest paid, but the wealth never created.

Furthermore, his debt obligations were forcing him to delay other wealth-building activities. Without his bad debt payments, Michael could max out his retirement accounts, build a real estate investment portfolio, or fund a business venture—all paths to significant wealth accumulation that remained closed while he serviced his consumer debt.

The Freedom Dividend: Benefits Beyond the Numbers

Liability reduction creates benefits beyond purely financial calculations:

1. **Enhanced cash flow flexibility:** Eliminating debt payments increases monthly discretionary income, creating options for investment or other opportunities.

2. **Improved risk resilience:** Lower fixed obligations mean greater ability to weather income disruptions or economic downturns.
3. **Expanded lifestyle options:** Without debt service requirements, options like career changes, location moves, or entrepreneurship become more accessible.
4. **Reduced financial stress:** The psychological burden of debt affects everything from sleep quality to relationship health to decision-making clarity.
5. **Greater negotiating power:** Minimal debt obligations strengthen your position in salary negotiations, business deals, and investment opportunities.

For Michael, understanding these comprehensive benefits strengthened his motivation to tackle his liability burden systematically.

The Strategic Liability Reduction Framework

With clarity about which debts are hindering wealth creation, the next step is implementing a systematic approach to liability reduction.

Phase 1: Debt Assessment and Categorization

Before developing a reduction strategy, complete a comprehensive inventory of all liabilities:

- **List all debts completely:**
    - Creditor name
    - Current balance

- Interest rate
- Minimum monthly payment
- Payment due date
- Secured/unsecured status
- Any special terms (e.g., deferment options, prepayment penalties)
- **Categorize each debt:**
    - Good debt (wealth-building)
    - Bad debt (wealth-draining)
    - Neutral debt (neither clearly good nor bad)
- **Calculate key metrics:**
    - Total debt amount
    - Total monthly debt obligations
    - Debt-to-income ratio (monthly debt payments divided by monthly gross income)
    - Weighted average interest rate

This assessment creates the foundation for a targeted reduction strategy.

Phase 2: Emergency Stabilization (If Needed)

If your debt situation has reached crisis level (payments being missed, collectors calling, legal action threatened), implement these emergency measures before proceeding:

1. **Prioritize essential secured debt:** Maintain payments on mortgages, auto loans, and other secured debt to prevent repossession or foreclosure.

2. **Contact creditors proactively:** Reach out before missing payments to discuss hardship options, which might include:
   - Temporary payment reductions
   - Interest rate modifications
   - Short-term forbearance
   - Payment date adjustments to align with income
3. **Consider professional assistance:** If the situation is severe, consult with:
   - Non-profit credit counseling agencies
   - Debt management programs
   - In extreme cases, bankruptcy attorneys to understand all options
4. **Implement drastic temporary measures:** Consider radical short-term lifestyle adjustments to create financial breathing room:
   - Temporary housing changes to reduce costs
   - Transportation downgrades
   - Extreme discretionary spending cuts
   - Additional income sources, even if temporary

Phase 3: Strategic Debt Elimination Plan

Once stabilized (or if not in crisis initially), implement a systematic elimination strategy for bad debt:

Option A: The Avalanche Method (Mathematically Optimal)

- List debts in order of interest rate, highest to lowest
- Pay minimum payments on all debts
- Direct all additional funds to the highest-interest debt

CHAPTER 5: DIMINISH LIABILITIES

- Once highest-interest debt is eliminated, roll that payment to the next highest
- Continue until all targeted debts are eliminated

Option B: The Snowball Method (Psychologically Powerful)

- List debts in order of balance, smallest to largest
- Pay minimum payments on all debts
- Direct all additional funds to the smallest balance
- Once smallest debt is eliminated, roll that payment to the next smallest
- Continue until all targeted debts are eliminated

Option C: The Hybrid Method (Balanced Approach)

- Start with the snowball method for quick wins and motivation
- Transition to the avalanche method after eliminating 2-3 small debts
- Consider prioritizing debts causing significant stress regardless of balance or rate

Acceleration Strategies for Any Method:

- Allocate all windfalls (tax refunds, bonuses, gifts) to debt reduction
- Implement a temporary "spending fast" to increase debt payment capacity
- Consider a side hustle dedicated solely to debt elimination
- Sell underutilized assets and apply proceeds to debt

- Automate increased payments to avoid decision fatigue and temptation

For Michael, we implemented the hybrid approach. He started by eliminating two small credit card balances ($3,200 and $4,500) using the snowball method, creating momentum and psychological wins. Then he transitioned to the avalanche method, targeting his highest-interest debts systematically.

Strategic Debt Restructuring: Optimization Without Elimination

In some cases, restructuring debt can create significant advantages even without immediate payoff:

1. Mortgage Refinancing

When interest rates drop significantly or your credit improves, refinancing your mortgage can create substantial monthly savings and lifetime interest reduction.

Implementation strategy:

- Consider refinancing when you can reduce your rate by at least 0.75-1%
- Calculate the breakeven point (how long it takes for monthly savings to offset closing costs)
- Avoid extending your loan term significantly unless absolutely necessary

- Consider rate-and-term refinances rather than cash-out options when focused on liability reduction
- Shop multiple lenders to find optimal terms

2. Debt Consolidation

Combining multiple high-interest debts into a single lower-interest loan can reduce both monthly payments and total interest paid.

Implementation strategy:

- Consider personal loans from credit unions or online lenders for unsecured debt consolidation
- Explore home equity loans or lines of credit for larger consolidation needs (with caution)
- Calculate the all-in interest rate and fees compared to your current situation
- Avoid consolidation offers with hidden fees, prepayment penalties, or balloon payments
- Most importantly: address the underlying spending issues that created the debt to avoid re-accumulation

3. Balance Transfer Strategies

Credit card balance transfers can provide temporary 0% interest periods, creating a window for accelerated payoff.

Implementation strategy:

- Look for offers with 0% terms of 12-18 months and minimal transfer fees (under 3%)
- Calculate whether the fee is worth the interest savings based on your payoff timeline
- Create a structured payoff plan to eliminate the balance before the promotional period ends
- Avoid making new purchases on the balance transfer card
- Set calendar reminders for when the promotional period ends

4. Student Loan Optimization

Federal student loans offer multiple repayment and forgiveness options that can significantly impact your overall financial picture.

Implementation strategy:

- Evaluate income-driven repayment plans if struggling with payments
- Consider refinancing private student loans when interest rates decline
- Explore loan forgiveness programs based on your profession and employer
- Understand the tax implications of different repayment and forgiveness options
- For those working in public service, ensure your employment qualifies for Public Service Loan Forgiveness

5. Strategic Settlement

For accounts already in collections or severe delinquency, negotiated settlements may reduce your overall liability.

Implementation strategy:

- Understand the impact on your credit score before proceeding
- Get all settlement agreements in writing before making payments
- Negotiate removal of negative credit reporting when possible ("pay for delete")
- Understand the potential tax implications—forgiven debt over $600 may be taxable as income
- Consider professional assistance for complex settlement negotiations

For Michael, strategic debt restructuring created immediate benefits. He:

- Refinanced his primary home mortgage, reducing his rate from 4.5% to 3.1%
- Consolidated $32,000 in credit card debt using a personal loan at 9.9% (down from an average of 22%)
- Transferred the balance from his highest-rate card (26.99%) to a 0% offer for 18 months
- Restructured his student loans into an income-driven repayment plan

These moves reduced his monthly debt obligations by approximately $1,200 while also reducing his long-term interest costs—freeing up capital for his debt elimination plan.

Leveraging Good Debt: Strategic Borrowing for Wealth Building

While eliminating bad debt accelerates wealth building, strategic use of good debt can actually amplify it. Understanding when and how to use leverage is a key differentiator between those who build modest wealth and those who build significant wealth.

The Power of Leverage in Wealth Building

Leverage—using borrowed money to increase your investment capacity—creates several advantages when used responsibly:

1. **Asset control amplification:** Allows control of larger assets than would be possible with cash alone
2. **Returns magnification:** Enhances percentage returns on your invested capital when asset performance exceeds borrowing costs
3. **Inflation benefit:** Fixed-rate debt becomes effectively cheaper over time as inflation erodes the real value of the debt
4. **Tax efficiency:** Interest on debt used for investment purposes is often tax-deductible, reducing the effective cost of borrowing
5. **Capital preservation:** Allows maintenance of liquid reserves and investment positions rather than liquidating for purchases

CHAPTER 5: DIMINISH LIABILITIES

Strategic Good Debt Applications

Consider these wealth-building applications of strategic borrowing:

1. Real Estate Investment Leverage

Perhaps the most accessible form of wealth-building leverage, real estate investment debt can create significant advantages.

Implementation strategy:

- Utilize conventional financing for initial investments (typically 20-25% down payment)
- As equity builds, consider cash-out refinancing to acquire additional properties
- Implement the BRRRR strategy (Buy, Rehab, Rent, Refinance, Repeat) to recycle capital
- Maintain adequate cash reserves to cover potential vacancies and repairs
- Ensure each property maintains positive cash flow even with debt service

2. Business Acquisition and Expansion

Debt financing for business purposes can create substantial returns when the business generates ROI exceeding borrowing costs.

Implementation strategy:

- Consider SBA loans for business acquisitions (typically 10-20% down payment)
- Utilize equipment financing to preserve working capital for operations and growth
- Implement lines of credit for inventory expansion and seasonal working capital needs
- Structure debt with terms matching the lifecycle of what's being financed
- Maintain debt service coverage ratios above 1.25 for financial stability

3. Investment Portfolio Leverage

Used carefully, investment portfolio leverage can enhance returns in certain market conditions.

Implementation strategy:

- Consider securities-backed lines of credit (SBLOCs) rather than margin loans for longer-term strategies
- Maintain conservative loan-to-value ratios (typically under 50%) to prevent margin calls
- Apply leverage strategically during market corrections rather than peaks
- Implement strict risk management protocols, including predetermined exit points
- Avoid leveraging already-volatile investments, which compounds risk

4. Education as Investment

When education substantially increases earning potential, education debt can represent an investment rather than a liability.

Implementation strategy:

- Calculate the ROI by comparing total costs against the projected income increase
- Prioritize programs with demonstrated placement rates and alumni success
- Consider cash-flowing the education when possible through part-time work or employer benefits
- Maximize scholarships, grants, and federal loans before considering private loans
- Create a post-graduation repayment strategy before taking on the debt

Michael implemented several of these strategies as his bad debt diminished. He:

- Refinanced his rental property to acquire a second investment property
- Established a home equity line of credit on his primary residence with a clear plan to use it only for investment opportunities
- Structured a small business loan to launch a consulting practice related to his expertise

These strategic uses of good debt accelerated his wealth-building significantly, creating assets and income streams that far exceeded the cost of the associated liabilities.

Debt Recycling: The Advanced Strategy

For those who have eliminated bad debt and mastered basic leverage, debt recycling represents an advanced strategy that can significantly accelerate wealth building.

The Debt Recycling Concept

Debt recycling involves systematically converting non-deductible debt (like your home mortgage) into deductible debt used for investment purposes. This strategy:

1. Creates tax deductions that effectively reduce borrowing costs
2. Builds investment assets while maintaining the original asset (e.g., your home)
3. Eventually results in both a paid-off original asset and a substantial investment portfolio

CHAPTER 5: DIMINISH LIABILITIES

Implementation Framework

While specific implementation varies based on individual circumstances, the general process follows these steps:

1. **Establish an investment line of credit,** either through a home equity line or by restructuring your primary mortgage to include an accessible portion.
2. **Draw from this credit line to make investments** in income-producing assets (typically dividend-paying stocks, ETFs, or investment properties).
3. **Use the investment income plus any additional capacity** to make payments on the original debt.
4. **As principal is paid down on the original debt, draw that amount again** and make additional investments.
5. **Repeat this cycle until the original debt is eliminated** and you own both the original asset and a substantial investment portfolio.

This strategy works best when:

- The investment return exceeds the borrowing cost (after tax considerations)
- You maintain stable income to support the debt service
- You have a long-term perspective (typically 10+ years)
- You implement proper risk management strategies
- You work with qualified tax professionals to ensure compliance

For Michael, we implemented a modified debt recycling strategy once his bad debt was eliminated. He established a home equity line of credit, then systematically drew from it to invest in dividend-focused ETFs. The dividends, along with additional contributions, were used to pay down his primary mortgage. As principal reduction occurred, he drew the equivalent amount to make additional investments. This structured approach put him on track to own both his home outright and a substantial investment portfolio within 12 years.

Expanding the "Buy, Borrow, Die" Strategy through Asset-Backed Borrowing

As introduced in the previous chapter, the "Buy, Borrow, Die" strategy represents one of the most powerful approaches used by wealthy families to preserve and grow assets while maintaining liquidity.

Strategic Implementation at Various Wealth Levels

This approach can be implemented at different scales depending on your asset base:

Beginning Wealth Stage (Net Worth $100K-$500K)

Implementation strategy:

- Establish a home equity line of credit once you have sufficient equity
- Maintain the HELOC with zero or minimal balance until needed
- Use selectively for high-ROI investments or opportunities rather than consumption

- Implement strict repayment plans when the line is used
- Begin building diversified assets that can later support additional borrowing capacity

Intermediate Wealth Stage (Net Worth $500K-$2M)

Implementation strategy:

- Establish both real estate and securities-backed lines of credit
- Structure real estate investments to maintain borrowing capacity through equity
- Begin implementing portfolio loans against investment accounts once they reach sufficient size
- Consider cash value life insurance as an additional asset-backed borrowing base
- Develop relationships with private bankers who can facilitate asset-backed lending

Advanced Wealth Stage (Net Worth $2M+)

Implementation strategy:

- Implement a coordinated asset-backed borrowing strategy across multiple asset classes
- Establish banking relationships that provide preferred lending terms based on overall asset base
- Consider private banking arrangements that offer portfolio-based lines of credit

- Implement family office strategies that optimize borrowing across family assets
- Integrate with estate planning for maximum multigenerational efficiency

The key to successful implementation at any level is ensuring that borrowed funds are used for either:

1. Acquiring additional appreciating assets, or
2. Addressing needs that would otherwise require liquidating existing assets

Asset-Backed Borrowing Vehicles

Several financial vehicles facilitate this strategy:

Home Equity Lines of Credit (HELOCs)

Advantages:

- Relatively low interest rates (typically prime plus a margin)
- Flexible access through checks, cards, or electronic transfers
- Interest may be tax-deductible when used for qualifying purposes
- Typically no costs to maintain when not in use

Implementation considerations:

- Typically limited to 80-85% of home value minus existing mortgages

- Usually variable interest rates, creating some uncertainty
- Potential for reduction or freezing during economic downturns
- Property serves as collateral, creating some risk

Securities-Backed Lines of Credit (SBLOCs)

Advantages:

- Often lower rates than HELOCs due to liquid collateral
- No application fees or closing costs in most cases
- No set repayment schedule (interest-only options)
- Does not appear on credit reports in many cases

Implementation considerations:

- Typically limited to 50-70% of portfolio value depending on composition
- Margin call risk if portfolio values decline significantly
- Not available for retirement accounts due to regulatory restrictions
- Cannot be used to purchase additional securities in most cases

Life Insurance Policy Loans

Advantages:

- No qualification requirements beyond sufficient cash value
- No fixed repayment schedule (can even be repaid by death benefit)

- Policy continues growing even with outstanding loans (in many designs)
- Completely private transactions not reported to credit bureaus

Implementation considerations:

- Requires properly structured permanent life insurance with sufficient cash value
- Reduces death benefit if not repaid
- Can create tax consequences if policy lapses with outstanding loans
- Often higher interest rates than other asset-backed options

Business Lines of Credit

Advantages:

- Can be secured by business assets rather than personal assets
- Often higher limits than personal borrowing options
- Interest is generally tax-deductible as a business expense
- Builds business credit history separate from personal credit

Implementation considerations:

- Typically requires personal guarantees until business reaches substantial size
- May require specific collateral depending on business type and size
- Often requires regular renewal and review

- May include covenants requiring maintenance of certain financial ratios

For Michael, implementing these strategies became possible as his wealth grew. Three years into his journey, having eliminated all bad debt and built significant assets, he had established:

- A $200,000 HELOC on his primary residence
- A $75,000 securities-backed line against his investment portfolio
- A properly structured whole life insurance policy with growing borrowing capacity

These tools gave him access to capital without liquidating growth assets—a cornerstone of the "Buy, Borrow, Die" approach.

The Psychology of Debt Mastery

Beyond the mechanics of liability reduction and strategic borrowing lies the equally important psychological dimension. Mastering this aspect is often what separates those who create lasting wealth from those who remain trapped in cycles of debt accumulation.

Healing Dysfunctional Money Patterns

Many debt challenges stem from underlying psychological patterns:

1. **Status anxiety:** Using debt to finance a lifestyle that projects success before actually achieving it

2. **Scarcity mindset:** Panic buying or hoarding behaviors that lead to excessive consumption on credit
3. **Instant gratification conditioning:** Difficulty delaying purchases until they can be afforded with cash
4. **Financial trauma responses:** Using spending to self-soothe after past financial hardships or instability
5. **Identity attachment:** Associating self-worth with specific possessions or experiences that require debt

Addressing these patterns often requires:

- Identifying specific triggers for problematic spending
- Developing alternative responses to emotional triggers
- Creating systems that introduce pause before purchasing
- Redefining success and worth independent of consumption
- In some cases, working with financial therapists who specialize in these issues

For Michael, status anxiety and identity attachment were primary drivers of his debt accumulation. His luxury car, boat, and excessive home represented attempts to project success to others and himself. Working through these patterns was essential to his financial transformation.

Building Healthy Debt Mindsets

Beyond healing dysfunctional patterns, developing proactive healthy mindsets creates lasting change:

1. **Strategic perspective:** Viewing debt as a tool that should provide clear, measurable benefits exceeding its costs

2. **Opportunity cost awareness:** Automatically calculating what borrowed money could earn if invested instead
3. **Future-self empathy:** Making decisions with consideration for your future financial well-being
4. **Value-based assessment:** Evaluating purchases based on alignment with core values rather than status or temporary pleasure
5. **Wealth stewardship:** Recognizing that financial resources represent opportunity and impact potential, not just consumption capacity

Developing these mindsets transforms the entire experience of making financial decisions, creating natural resistance to wealth-draining debt while enabling strategic use of wealth-building debt.

Liability Reduction Systems and Automation

Successful liability reduction isn't just about strategy—it's about implementing systems that make execution automatic and consistent.

The Debt Freedom System

Consider implementing these elements as a comprehensive system:

1. **Automated tracking:** Implement apps or systems that automatically update balances and payments, providing clear visibility.
2. **Progress visualization:** Create visually compelling representations of your debt reduction journey to maintain motivation.

3. **Automated extra payments:** Set up automatic transfers that apply additional principal payments without requiring ongoing decisions.
4. **Windfall routing protocols:** Establish pre-determined allocations for any unexpected income, removing in-the-moment decision making.
5. **Accountability structures:** Implement regular check-ins with partners, financial advisors, or accountability groups to maintain commitment.
6. **Celebration milestones:** Define specific achievements that trigger predetermined (non-financial) rewards, reinforcing progress.
7. **Debt-free vision connection:** Maintain visible reminders of what your life will look like once free from debt obligations.
8. **Financial maintenance calendar:** Schedule regular reviews of debt reduction progress, refinancing opportunities, and strategy adjustments.

For Michael, automation proved particularly effective. He established automatic extra payments toward his highest-interest debt, created a visual debt reduction tracker on his refrigerator, and implemented "first-dollar allocation rules" that automatically routed any unexpected income.

"The systems made all the difference," Michael reflected. "On days when motivation was low, the automation kept me moving forward without requiring a new decision."

The Family Liability Strategy

For Black families building generational wealth, a coordinated approach to liability management creates substantial advantages for current and future generations.

Cross-Generational Liability Management

Consider these strategies for family-wide implementation:

1. **Family financial education:** Implement age-appropriate education about debt, credit, and leverage for all family members.
2. **Debt avoidance protocols:** Establish family guidelines for when debt is appropriate and when alternatives should be pursued.
3. **Strategic liability support:** Consider targeted support for good debt that advances family wealth-building (education, business, real estate) while avoiding enabling bad debt accumulation.
4. **Financial emergency planning:** Create family-wide protocols for handling financial emergencies without destructive debt.
5. **Legacy liability protection:** Implement estate planning that prevents assets from being consumed by liabilities across generations.
6. **Family wealth mission alignment:** Ensure all borrowing decisions align with the family's broader wealth mission and values.

For the Richardson family we advised, implementing these strategies transformed their cross-generational approach to debt. When their daughter needed funding for graduate school, instead of traditional student loans, they implemented a family financing arrangement that kept interest payments within the family while providing better terms than commercial options. Their son's business venture was funded through a combination of family investment and strategically structured outside financing that preserved both control and growth potential.

"We've completely reimagined how our family thinks about debt," Mr. Richardson shared. "Instead of seeing it as solely negative, we view it as one tool in our family wealth strategy—to be used carefully and strategically when it truly advances our collective goals."

Michael: Four Years Later

Let's revisit Michael's journey four years after implementing his liability reduction and strategic borrowing plan.

His transformation has been remarkable:

Bad Debt Elimination:

- All credit card debt eliminated
- Both luxury vehicles replaced with one modest, reliable car (purchased with cash)
- Boat sold, eliminating that loan entirely
- Personal loans fully paid off

Good Debt Optimization:

- Primary residence mortgage refinanced at lower rate, with accelerated payment plan

- Rental property performing well with positive cash flow after all expenses
- Student loans on income-driven repayment plan
- Two additional investment properties acquired with strategic financing

Asset-Backed Borrowing Implementation:

- HELOC established for investment opportunities
- Securities-backed line available but rarely used
- Whole life policy with growing cash value and borrowing capacity

Financial Position Transformation:

- Debt-to-income ratio reduced from 60% to 25%
- Investment portfolio grown to over $350,000
- Monthly cash flow improved by over $3,000
- On track for financial independence within 8 years

Perhaps most importantly, Michael's relationship with debt has fundamentally changed. He now views it as a strategic tool rather than a way to finance lifestyle, making borrowing decisions based on careful analysis rather than emotional impulse.

"I used to think wealth was about what you could buy," Michael reflected. "Now I understand it's about what you own and control. Strategic borrowing helps me own and control more assets that generate income and grow in value."

Your Liability Mastery Journey

As we conclude this chapter, remember that mastering liabilities—both eliminating the destructive ones and strategically using the constructive ones—represents a critical milestone on your wealth-building journey.

Whether you're currently overwhelmed with debt like Michael was initially, or simply looking to optimize your liability strategy, the principles in this chapter provide a roadmap for transformation. Start where you are, implement one strategy at a time, and watch as your financial landscape changes.

For Black families building generational wealth, liability mastery creates particularly significant advantages. By eliminating the drain of bad debt and strategically using good debt, we can accelerate asset acquisition and wealth building, helping to close the persistent racial wealth gap while creating new possibilities for current and future generations.

In the next chapter, we'll explore how to amplify your wealth through strategic investments across multiple asset classes. But first, complete the action steps below to begin your liability mastery journey.

CHAPTER 5: DIMINISH LIABILITIES

ACTION STEP: List All Liabilities and Create a Debt Elimination Plan

- ☐ **Complete your liability inventory**
    - ☐ List all debts with balances, interest rates, and monthly payments
    - ☐ Categorize each as good debt, bad debt, or neutral
    - ☐ Calculate your total debt burden
    - ☐ Determine your current debt-to-income ratio
- ☐ **Create your bad debt elimination plan**
    - ☐ Select your elimination method (avalanche, snowball, or hybrid)
    - ☐ List debts in the appropriate priority order
    - ☐ Calculate how much extra you can apply to debt elimination monthly
    - ☐ Project payoff dates for each debt
    - ☐ Identify specific acceleration strategies you'll implement
- ☐ **Develop your debt optimization strategy**
    - ☐ Identify opportunities to restructure existing debt advantageously
    - ☐ Research specific refinancing or consolidation options
    - ☐ Calculate potential monthly and lifetime savings from optimization
    - ☐ Determine which options to pursue and in what order

- ☐ **Design your strategic borrowing framework**
    - ☐ Identify potential good debt applications for your wealth-building goals
    - ☐ Research specific lending options and terms
    - ☐ Define clear criteria for when you'll utilize strategic borrowing
    - ☐ Establish risk management protocols for leveraged investments
- ☐ **Implement your automation system**
    - ☐ Set up automatic tracking for all liabilities
    - ☐ Create your visual progress tracker
    - ☐ Schedule automatic extra payments
    - ☐ Establish your financial maintenance calendar with regular review dates

Remember: Liability mastery isn't about eliminating all debt—it's about eliminating wealth-draining debt while strategically using wealth-building debt. The goal is ensuring every dollar of interest paid creates more value than it costs.

CHAPTER 6

AMPLIFY INVESTMENTS

"The best time to plant a tree was 20 years ago. The second best time is now."
—Chinese Proverb

"I've been playing it safe my entire life, and now I realize I've been playing it too safe."

This realization came from Janet, a 46-year-old healthcare administrator who sought our guidance after decades of following conventional financial wisdom. She had done everything "right" according to traditional advice: maintained steady employment, lived below her means, avoided debt, and saved consistently. She had accumulated nearly $180,000 in a savings account, earning minimal interest.

"I thought I was being responsible," Janet explained. "My parents lost everything in bad investments when I was young, so I've always been terrified of losing my money. But now I understand that my 'safe' approach has actually been costing me hundreds of thousands in missed growth."

Janet's situation highlights a common obstacle on the journey to building wealth: the failure to transform savings into investments that grow substantially over time. This critical transition—from merely accumulating to strategically growing wealth—is why "Amplify Investments" is the sixth step in our Abundance Formula.

The Investment Imperative: Why Saving Alone Isn't Enough

For generations, financial stability in many Black families has been defined primarily by the ability to pay bills, avoid debt, and perhaps maintain an emergency fund. While these foundations are essential, they're insufficient for building significant wealth.

The Hidden Cost of "Safety"

What many perceive as financial safety—keeping money in savings accounts, certificates of deposit, or other "guaranteed" vehicles—actually carries a significant hidden cost: the erosion of purchasing power through inflation and the opportunity cost of foregone growth.

To understand this cost, consider Janet's situation. Her $180,000 in savings, accumulated over 20 years of disciplined saving, was earning 0.5% interest while inflation averaged around 2.5%. This meant her money was effectively losing 2% of its purchasing power annually. Had she invested this money in a diversified portfolio earning a conservative 8% average annual return, her nest egg would have grown to approximately $825,000—a difference of $645,000.

This "safety tax" is particularly devastating for Black families building wealth, as it compounds the effects of other historical barriers to wealth accumulation. When starting from behind due to systemic factors, we cannot afford strategies that actually move us backward in real terms.

The Investment Mindset Shift

Building wealth requires a fundamental shift in thinking about money:

From:

- Money as something to be preserved and protected
- Success measured by what you've saved
- Risk seen as something to be avoided entirely
- Financial decisions driven primarily by fear
- Focus on preventing loss

To:

- Money as a tool to be deployed strategically
- Success measured by what your money earns for you
- Risk understood as something to be managed, not avoided
- Financial decisions driven by calculated opportunity
- Focus on creating growth while managing downside

This mindset shift doesn't mean abandoning prudence or embracing recklessness. Rather, it means developing a sophisticated understanding of how wealth is actually built over time—through the careful but deliberate assumption of appropriate risk for commensurate reward.

Understanding the Investment Spectrum

Before developing your investment strategy, it's essential to understand the full spectrum of investment options and their risk-return characteristics.

The Risk-Return Relationship

At the heart of investment theory is the relationship between risk and return: generally, the higher the potential return, the higher the risk. But this relationship is more nuanced than many realize:

1. **Risk varies by time horizon:** Investments considered "risky" in the short term often become significantly less risky over longer time frames.
2. **Risk is multidimensional:** Beyond just volatility, risk includes liquidity risk, inflation risk, concentration risk, and many other factors.
3. **Risk can be managed:** Through diversification, position sizing, and other strategies, many risks can be significantly reduced without proportionately reducing return potential.
4. **"Risk-free" options carry hidden risks:** What seems safest (like cash) actually guarantees loss of purchasing power in inflationary environments.

CHAPTER 6: AMPLIFY INVESTMENTS

The Investment Spectrum Overview

Let's examine the major investment categories across the risk-return spectrum:

Cash and Cash Equivalents

- **Examples:** Savings accounts, money market accounts, Treasury bills
- **Potential Return:** 0-2% historically
- **Risk Characteristics:** Minimal principal risk but high inflation risk
- **Appropriate Uses:** Emergency funds, short-term goals (0-2 years), temporary holdings between investments

Fixed Income

- **Examples:** Bonds (government, municipal, corporate), CDs, fixed annuities
- **Potential Return:** 2-5% historically
- **Risk Characteristics:** Lower volatility than stocks but interest rate risk, credit risk, and inflation risk
- **Appropriate Uses:** Income generation, capital preservation for intermediate goals (2-7 years), portfolio stabilization

Public Equities

- **Examples:** Individual stocks, mutual funds, ETFs, index funds
- **Potential Return:** 7-10% historically (U.S. market average)

- **Risk Characteristics:** Higher short-term volatility but strong long-term growth potential
- **Appropriate Uses:** Long-term growth (7+ years), wealth building, inflation protection

Real Estate

- **Examples:** Rental properties, REITs, real estate funds, crowdfunding
- **Potential Return:** 7-12% historically (including appreciation and income)
- **Risk Characteristics:** Moderate volatility, illiquidity, management requirements, but strong inflation protection
- **Appropriate Uses:** Long-term wealth building, income generation, portfolio diversification, inflation hedging

Private Investments

- **Examples:** Private equity, venture capital, angel investing, private lending
- **Potential Return:** 10-20%+ historically (highly variable)
- **Risk Characteristics:** High illiquidity, concentration risk, and potential for total loss, but also potential for outsized returns
- **Appropriate Uses:** Long-term wealth building for accredited investors, portfolio diversification, access to unique opportunities

CHAPTER 6: AMPLIFY INVESTMENTS

Alternative Investments

- **Examples:** Commodities, cryptocurrency, collectibles, structured products
- **Potential Return:** Highly variable (can range from negative to 100%+)
- **Risk Characteristics:** Often high volatility, specialized knowledge requirements, evolving regulatory landscapes
- **Appropriate Uses:** Portfolio diversification, specific strategic objectives, specialized opportunities

Understanding this spectrum allows you to place different investments in their proper context and make allocation decisions aligned with your specific goals, time horizon, and risk tolerance.

Building Your Investment Foundation: The Core Portfolio

For most wealth builders, a core investment portfolio should form the foundation of their investment strategy. This portfolio—typically focused on stocks, bonds, and perhaps REITs—provides broad market exposure, significant growth potential, and relative accessibility.

Key Principles of Successful Portfolio Construction

Regardless of your specific allocation, these principles should guide your approach:

1. Diversification Across and Within Asset Classes

Diversification—not putting all your eggs in one basket—remains one of the most powerful risk management tools available to investors.

Implementation strategy:

- Diversify across asset classes (stocks, bonds, real estate, etc.)
- Within each asset class, diversify across sectors, geographies, and company sizes
- Consider correlation between holdings—true diversification means assets that don't always move together
- Rebalance periodically to maintain your target diversification

2. Cost Minimization

Investment costs compound just like returns—but in the opposite direction. Minimizing costs significantly impacts long-term results.

Implementation strategy:

- Favor low-cost index funds and ETFs for core positions
- Be particularly cost-conscious for efficient market segments (like large-cap U.S. stocks)

CHAPTER 6: AMPLIFY INVESTMENTS

- Consider costs beyond just expense ratios (transaction costs, tax efficiency, etc.)
- Negotiate fees when working with advisors, and understand all costs involved

3. Tax Efficiency

Strategic tax management can significantly increase your effective returns without increasing risk.

Implementation strategy:

- Maximize tax-advantaged accounts (401(k)s, IRAs, HSAs, etc.)
- Place tax-inefficient investments (bonds, REITs) in tax-advantaged accounts when possible
- Consider tax-managed funds and ETFs for taxable accounts
- Implement tax-loss harvesting during market downturns
- When appropriate, consider municipal bonds for tax-free income

4. Appropriate Time Horizon Matching

Different investments are suitable for different time horizons, and matching them appropriately reduces unnecessary risk.

Implementation strategy:

- Define specific time horizons for each financial goal
- Align investment allocations with these horizons
- Increase conservative allocations as goals approach

- Maintain growth assets for longer-term objectives even during market volatility

5. Evidence-Based Strategy

Successful investing requires distinguishing between evidence-based approaches and market noise or speculation.

Implementation strategy:

- Base core strategies on academically validated investment principles
- Be skeptical of "hot tips," market timing claims, and guaranteed returns
- Understand the difference between investing and speculation
- Focus on factors with demonstrated long-term efficacy (value, quality, momentum, etc.)

Core Portfolio Models

While personalization is important, these model portfolios provide starting frameworks based on risk tolerance and time horizon:

Conservative Core Portfolio (Lower Risk, Shorter Horizon)

- 40% Total Stock Market Index
- 40% Total Bond Market Index
- 10% International Stock Index
- 10% Short-Term Treasury Bonds or TIPS

- **Expected Historical Return:** 5-7% annually

Moderate Core Portfolio (Balanced Risk, Medium Horizon)

- 50% Total Stock Market Index
- 20% International Stock Index
- 20% Total Bond Market Index
- 10% REIT Index
- **Expected Historical Return:** 7-9% annually

Growth Core Portfolio (Higher Risk, Longer Horizon)

- 60% Total Stock Market Index
- 25% International Stock Index
- 10% Small Cap Value Index
- 5% Total Bond Market Index
- **Expected Historical Return:** 8-10% annually

Aggressive Growth Core Portfolio (High Risk, Long Horizon)

- 50% Total Stock Market Index
- 30% International Stock Index
- 15% Small Cap Value Index
- 5% Emerging Markets Index
- **Expected Historical Return:** 9-11% annually

For Janet, we recommended starting with the Moderate Core Portfolio given her age and goals. To address her fear of market volatility, we implemented a dollar-cost averaging strategy, gradually moving her savings into investments over 18 months rather than all at once. This approach helped her manage the psychological transition while still capturing growth potential.

Real Estate Investment Strategies

While public market investments form an important foundation, real estate investing has created more millionaires than perhaps any other asset class. For Black families building wealth, real estate offers particular advantages: tangibility, inflation protection, tax benefits, and the ability to use leverage effectively.

Core Real Estate Investment Approaches

Consider these accessible approaches to real estate investing:

1. Residential Rental Properties

Purchasing homes or small multi-family properties to rent to tenants combines appreciation potential with ongoing income.

Implementation strategy:

- Start with single-family homes or duplexes in stable neighborhoods
- Focus on cash flow first, appreciation second
- Implement the 1% rule (monthly rent should be at least 1% of purchase price) when possible

- Build a team including property manager, maintenance contractors, and real estate attorney
- Consider "house hacking" (living in one unit of a multi-unit property) as an entry point

2. Real Estate Investment Trusts (REITs)

These publicly traded companies own, operate, or finance income-producing real estate, providing real estate exposure without direct property management.

Implementation strategy:

- Consider both broad REIT index funds and specialized REITs in sectors like healthcare, data centers, or residential
- Understand the difference between equity REITs (which own properties) and mortgage REITs (which finance real estate)
- Hold REITs in tax-advantaged accounts when possible due to their tax-inefficient income
- Use REITs for diversification and income rather than maximum growth
- Consider both publicly traded REITs and non-traded REITs for different objectives

3. Real Estate Crowdfunding

Online platforms now allow fractional investment in commercial and residential properties with much lower minimums than traditional commercial real estate.

Implementation strategy:

- Research platforms carefully (Fundrise, RealtyMogul, and CrowdStreet are established options)
- Start small to understand the process and platform
- Diversify across multiple projects rather than concentrating in one
- Understand liquidity limitations—most investments are tied up for 3-7 years
- Consider both debt and equity crowdfunding investments for different risk-return profiles

4. Real Estate Wholesaling and Flipping

For those willing to be more active, identifying undervalued properties and either assigning contracts to other investors (wholesaling) or renovating and reselling (flipping) can generate significant returns.

Implementation strategy:

- Develop systems for finding undervalued properties
- Build relationships with contractors, investors, and real estate agents
- Start with straightforward projects before tackling major renovations
- Calculate all costs thoroughly before committing to projects
- Create standardized analysis models to evaluate opportunities quickly

5. Commercial Real Estate

As your portfolio grows, commercial properties (retail, office, industrial, self-storage) can provide stronger leases, higher-quality tenants, and often better cash flow than residential.

Implementation strategy:

- Consider starting with simple commercial properties like single-tenant retail or small office buildings
- Understand the different lease structures (especially triple-net leases)
- Build relationships with commercial brokers and lenders
- Consider partnerships to pool capital for larger opportunities
- Develop expertise in specific commercial niches rather than trying to master all sectors

For Timothy, an engineer we advised who had built a strong stock portfolio but wanted more tangible investments, residential real estate provided an ideal complement. He started with a duplex in a stable neighborhood near a major hospital (ensuring tenant demand), living in one unit while renting the other. This "house hacking" approach reduced his living expenses while building equity and providing tax advantages. Within five years, he had expanded to owning four rental properties generating substantial positive cash flow alongside their appreciation.

Business Ownership and Private Investments

While public markets and real estate form the foundation of many wealth-building portfolios, business ownership and private investments often provide the highest potential returns, though with correspondingly higher risk and involvement requirements.

Business Ownership Strategies

Business ownership—whether starting a new venture or acquiring an existing one—remains one of the most direct paths to significant wealth creation.

1. Side Business Development

Starting a business while maintaining employment provides income stability with entrepreneurial upside.

Implementation strategy:

- Identify business opportunities aligned with your skills and market needs
- Start with minimal capital investment to test concepts
- Develop systems that allow operation within limited time availability
- Reinvest profits to fuel growth rather than increasing lifestyle
- Create clear metrics to determine when to scale or pivot

2. Business Acquisition

Purchasing an existing business can reduce startup risk while providing immediate cash flow.

CHAPTER 6: AMPLIFY INVESTMENTS

Implementation strategy:

- Focus on businesses with proven cash flow and established customer base
- Look for opportunities where the owner is retiring without succession plans
- Consider seller financing to reduce capital requirements
- Implement due diligence checklists covering financials, legal, operations, and market
- Identify specific improvement opportunities before acquisition

3. Franchise Investment

Franchising provides a middle ground between startup and acquisition, offering established systems with brand recognition.

Implementation strategy:

- Research franchise success rates and satisfaction within specific systems
- Understand total costs beyond just the franchise fee
- Speak with multiple current franchisees about their experience
- Consider semi-absentee models that don't require full-time involvement
- Evaluate territory protection and system growth trends

4. Professional Practice Development

For those with professional credentials, building a practice (medical, legal, accounting, etc.) combines professional income with business equity.

Implementation strategy:

- Focus on developing systems and team rather than just personal production
- Implement marketing strategies to reduce reliance on referrals
- Create standardized processes that don't require your personal involvement
- Consider acquisition of smaller practices for growth
- Develop exit strategies from early stages

Private Investment Strategies

Beyond your own business, investing in other private ventures can generate substantial returns and portfolio diversification.

1. Angel Investing

Direct investment in early-stage companies can produce exceptional returns when successful, though with high failure rates.

Implementation strategy:

- Join angel groups to access deal flow and collective due diligence
- Allocate only a small portion of portfolio (typically 5-10% maximum)
- Plan to make multiple investments rather than concentrating in one or two
- Develop expertise in specific sectors where you have knowledge advantage

- Consider convertible notes and SAFE agreements rather than just equity

2. Private Equity and Venture Capital Funds

These funds pool capital to invest in private companies at various stages, providing professional management and diversification.

Implementation strategy:

- Understand minimum investment requirements, which can be substantial
- Research fund manager track records and investment theses
- Consider funds-of-funds for additional diversification
- Be prepared for long lockup periods (often 7-10 years)
- Evaluate fee structures carefully (management fees and carried interest)

3. Private Lending

Providing loans to individuals or businesses can generate strong income with collateral protection.

Implementation strategy:

- Start with collateralized loans secured by real estate or business assets
- Implement proper legal documentation for all lending activities

- Consider lending through established platforms like PeerStreet for real estate or Funding Circle for businesses
- Diversify across multiple loans rather than concentrating exposure
- Establish clear protocols for managing defaults or workout situations

For Marcus, a technology executive with substantial public market investments, adding private investments provided both portfolio diversification and intellectual engagement. He joined an angel investor group focused on software startups, making small investments in 12 companies over three years. While several failed completely, one achieved a 15x return through acquisition, and two others showed strong growth potential. This portion of his portfolio, while small, provided uncorrelated returns and potential for outsized growth.

Strategic Asset Allocation: Building Your Complete Portfolio

With understanding of the major asset classes, the next step is developing a strategic allocation that aligns with your specific goals, time horizon, and risk tolerance.

CHAPTER 6: AMPLIFY INVESTMENTS

The Personal Portfolio Framework

Consider this framework for developing your comprehensive investment strategy:

Core Portfolio (50-70% of Assets)

The foundation of your investment approach, providing broad market exposure with relatively low costs and maintenance requirements.

Typical components:

- Broad market index funds and ETFs (U.S. and international stocks)
- Bond funds aligned with your risk tolerance
- REIT funds for real estate exposure
- Target-date or asset allocation funds in retirement accounts

Primary objectives: Long-term growth, diversification, inflation protection, tax efficiency

Strategic Portfolio (20-40% of Assets)

More targeted investments aligned with specific goals, themes, or opportunities you identify.

Typical components:

- Individual stocks in sectors you understand well
- Actively managed funds in less efficient markets
- Direct real estate investments

- Specific bonds or bond funds for income goals
- Dividend-focused investments for income
- Factor-based ETFs (value, quality, momentum)

Primary objectives: Enhanced returns, specific income needs, targeted opportunities, personal interests

Opportunistic Portfolio (5-15% of Assets)

Higher-risk, higher-potential-return investments that may have lower correlation with traditional markets.

Typical components:

- Private equity investments
- Venture capital
- Angel investments
- Cryptocurrency
- Specialized alternative investments
- Tactical trading strategies

Primary objectives: Potential outsized returns, portfolio diversification, participation in emerging trends

The exact allocation between these categories should be adjusted based on your:

- Age and investment time horizon
- Income stability and cash flow needs
- Risk tolerance, both emotional and financial
- Tax situation

- Specific financial goals
- Interest and expertise in different investment areas
- Access to specific opportunities

Strategic Allocation Adjustments

Your allocation strategy should evolve based on both market conditions and personal circumstances:

Age-Based Adjustments

Traditional wisdom suggests reducing risk as you age, but the relationship should be more nuanced:

Early accumulation phase (20s-30s):

- Higher allocation to growth assets (stocks, real estate, private investments)
- Minimal fixed income except for specific short-term goals
- Greater capacity to take calculated risks with longer recovery horizon

Prime accumulation phase (40s-50s):

- Still growth-oriented but with increased diversification
- Strategic fixed income for specific objectives
- More defined allocation among various investment categories

Pre-retirement phase (50s-60s):

- Increased focus on capital preservation but still maintaining growth exposure
- Development of income-producing assets
- More conservative opportunistic allocations

Distribution phase (retirement):

- Focus on reliable income generation
- Capital preservation for core needs
- Growth allocation for longevity protection
- Legacy planning considerations

Goal-Based Adjustments

Different goals require different investment approaches:

Retirement funding:

- Long-term horizon allows significant growth allocation
- Progressive shift toward income as retirement approaches
- Tax-advantaged accounts central to strategy

Education funding:

- Time horizon based on child's age
- 529 plans and other tax-advantaged approaches
- Significant reduction in risk as college approaches

CHAPTER 6: AMPLIFY INVESTMENTS

Major purchases (home, business):

- Clear time horizon dictates allocation
- Liquidity becomes increasingly important as goal approaches
- Lower risk tolerance than longer-term goals

Legacy/generational wealth:

- Very long time horizon allows maximum growth orientation
- Tax planning central to strategy
- Consideration of transfer mechanisms and structures

Market Condition Adjustments

Strategic shifts based on market environments:

During significant market overvaluation:

- Consider slight reduction in exposure to most extended areas
- Increase dry powder for future opportunities
- Maintain discipline with regular rebalancing

During significant market downturns:

- Maintain long-term allocations despite emotional challenges
- Consider strategic rebalancing into areas experiencing greatest decline
- Potentially accelerate planned contributions

During rising interest rate environments:

- Adjust bond duration strategy (typically shortening duration)
- Consider floating rate instruments
- Evaluate real estate holdings for interest rate sensitivity

During high inflation periods:

- Increase allocation to real assets (real estate, commodities)
- Consider TIPS and inflation-adjusted investments
- Evaluate businesses with pricing power

For Janet, we developed a comprehensive allocation strategy that addressed both her financial goals and her psychological comfort with investing. Her allocation included:

Core Portfolio (65%):

- 40% Total U.S. Stock Market Index
- 15% Total International Stock Index
- 10% Total Bond Market Index

Strategic Portfolio (30%):

- 15% Dividend Growth Fund
- 10% REIT Index Fund
- 5% Municipal Bond Fund (for tax-efficient income)

Opportunistic Portfolio (5%):

- 3% Real Estate Crowdfunding

- 2% Small angel investments through a platform

This balanced approach provided significant growth potential while incorporating income-generating assets that helped Janet feel more secure about her transition from saver to investor.

Using Liquidity from Credit Strategies to Amplify Investments

As discussed in previous chapters, strategic credit use can significantly enhance investment returns when properly implemented. Here we'll explore specific strategies for using credit to amplify investments while managing risk appropriately.

The Leverage Effect in Investment Returns

When investment returns exceed borrowing costs, leverage can substantially increase effective returns on your invested capital. However, leverage also amplifies losses when investments underperform, making risk management essential.

Consider this example:

- Investment: $100,000 property appreciating at 5% annually
- Without leverage: $5,000 gain on $100,000 investment
  = 5% return
- With 75% leverage ($25,000 down, $75,000 financed at 4%):
    - Appreciation: $5,000
    - Interest cost: $3,000

○   Net gain: $2,000 on $25,000 investment = 8% return

While the dollar gain is smaller, the percentage return on invested capital is significantly higher, allowing your capital to work more efficiently.

Strategic Credit Sources for Investment

Different credit sources offer varying advantages for investment amplification:

1. Securities-Backed Lines of Credit (SBLOCs)

These credit lines use your investment portfolio as collateral, typically offering favorable rates and flexible terms.

Implementation strategy:

- Maintain conservative loan-to-value ratios (typically 40-50% maximum)
- Use for opportunities with expected returns significantly exceeding borrowing costs
- Implement risk management protocols to prevent margin calls
- Consider for bridge financing in real estate or business acquisitions
- Typically available through brokerage firms with portfolios over $100,000

2. Home Equity Lines of Credit (HELOCs)

Leveraging your primary residence equity can provide accessible capital for investments.

Implementation strategy:

- Maintain total home debt (mortgage plus HELOC) below 80% of value
- Use for investments with relatively stable returns
- Consider potential tax advantages for interest when used for investments
- Implement as standby capital for opportunistic investments
- Particularly effective for real estate investments and business opportunities

3. Cash Value Life Insurance Policy Loans

Properly structured permanent life insurance can provide unique advantages as an investment funding source.

Implementation strategy:

- Design policies with reputable companies and minimal insurance costs
- Understand non-direct recognition vs. direct recognition policy differences
- Use primarily for opportunities with significant tax advantages
- Implement with no required repayment schedule (though repayment is generally advisable)

- Consider for investments where traditional financing is unavailable

4. Investment Property Refinancing

Extracting equity from existing investment properties to acquire additional assets can accelerate portfolio growth.

Implementation strategy:

- Maintain adequate equity buffers in all properties (typically 25%+)
- Ensure each property maintains positive cash flow after refinancing
- Use extracted capital only for additional investments, not consumption
- Consider during low interest rate environments
- Implement the BRRRR strategy (Buy, Rehab, Rent, Refinance, Repeat)

Risk Management with Leveraged Investments

The key to successful investment leverage is meticulous risk management:

1. **Maintain substantial liquidity reserves** when using leverage, ideally covering 6-12 months of all debt service obligations.
2. **Implement strict loan-to-value limits** for each asset type based on its volatility and liquidity.

3. **Stress test all leveraged investments** by calculating performance under adverse scenarios (declining values, rising interest rates, vacancy in real estate).
4. **Diversify both investment types and funding sources** to prevent system-wide risks.
5. **Create predetermined exit or deleveraging triggers** based on market conditions, personal circumstances, or investment performance.
6. **Consider fixed-rate financing for long-term investments** to eliminate interest rate risk, even at slightly higher initial rates.

For William, a physician we advised, strategic leverage transformed his investment trajectory. Using a combination of an SBLOC against his existing portfolio and a HELOC on his primary residence, he was able to acquire three cash-flowing rental properties without liquidating his retirement investments. The properties generated positive cash flow after all expenses, effectively paying down the borrowed principal while the properties appreciated—a double wealth-building effect that significantly accelerated his path to financial independence.

Advanced Investment Strategies

As your wealth grows and your investment sophistication increases, these advanced strategies can further enhance your portfolio's performance:

1. Tax-Loss Harvesting and Gain Management

Strategic realization of investment losses and gains can significantly improve after-tax returns without changing your overall investment allocation.

Implementation strategy:

- Identify investments with unrealized losses during market declines
- Sell these positions and replace with similar (but not "substantially identical") investments
- Use harvested losses to offset capital gains or up to $3,000 in ordinary income annually
- Carry forward additional losses for future years
- Coordinate with overall tax planning for optimal timing

2. Factor-Based Investing

Research has identified specific factors (value, size, momentum, quality, etc.) that have historically led to outperformance over long periods.

Implementation strategy:

- Implement through factor-specific ETFs or mutual funds

CHAPTER 6: AMPLIFY INVESTMENTS

- Consider multi-factor funds for diversification within this approach
- Understand factor cyclicality and maintain discipline during underperforming periods
- Consider factor tilts rather than pure factor portfolios
- Implement cost-efficiently through index-based products rather than active management

3. Alternative Income Strategies

Beyond traditional dividends and interest, these strategies can enhance portfolio income:

Implementation strategy:

- Consider covered call writing on existing equity positions
- Explore preferred stocks for higher income with moderate risk
- Implement bond ladders for predictable income streams
- Consider closed-end funds trading at discounts to net asset value
- Evaluate master limited partnerships (MLPs) for tax-advantaged income

4. Opportunistic Tactical Allocation

While market timing is generally counterproductive, certain significant market dislocations may present tactical opportunities.

Implementation strategy:

- Establish predetermined criteria for tactical shifts based on valuation metrics
- Implement modest adjustments rather than all-or-nothing moves
- Maintain core strategic allocation regardless of tactical positions
- Set specific exit criteria before implementing tactical positions
- Limit tactical allocation to a small portion of overall portfolio

5. Direct Indexing

This approach involves directly owning the individual components of an index rather than a fund, allowing for increased tax efficiency and customization.

Implementation strategy:

- Consider when portfolio size makes this cost-effective (typically $500,000+)
- Implement through specialized platforms or advisors offering this service
- Customize by excluding companies or sectors that conflict with your values
- Utilize for enhanced tax-loss harvesting opportunities
- Consider for coordination with concentrated positions or employer stock

These advanced strategies should complement rather than replace your core investment approach, adding incremental value to an already sound foundation.

Investment Implementation Systems

Even the best investment strategy fails without proper implementation systems. These systems ensure consistency, discipline, and efficiency in your investment process.

1. Automated Investment Programs

Automation removes emotion and inconsistency from the investment process.

Implementation strategy:

- Establish automatic transfers from income to investment accounts
- Implement automatic investment of accumulated cash into designated assets
- Consider dollar-cost averaging for new lump sums
- Automate reinvestment of dividends and interest
- Utilize automatic rebalancing features when available

2. Investment Policy Statements

This formal document defines your investment strategy, creating a framework for consistent decision-making.

Implementation elements:

- Overall financial goals and time horizons
- Target asset allocation with acceptable ranges
- Criteria for investment selection and removal
- Rebalancing triggers and methodology
- Performance benchmarks and review procedures
- Specific responsibilities (for self, advisors, or family members)

3. Regular Review Protocols

Systematic review processes ensure your investments remain aligned with your objectives.

Implementation elements:

- Scheduled comprehensive portfolio reviews (quarterly or semi-annually)
- Monthly monitoring of major positions or developments
- Annual tax planning related to investments
- Trigger-based reviews when major life events occur
- Documentation of all review findings and decisions

4. Education and Research Systems

Ongoing education enhances your ability to make sound investment decisions.

CHAPTER 6: AMPLIFY INVESTMENTS

Implementation elements:

- Curated information sources focused on long-term principles
- Regular reading schedule for investment education
- Participation in investment discussion groups or communities
- Documentation of lessons learned from both successes and mistakes
- Continuous development of investment knowledge in specific areas of interest

5. Record-Keeping Systems

Proper documentation is essential for tax compliance, performance evaluation, and decision improvement.

Implementation elements:

- Organized storage of all investment statements and tax documents
- Transaction logs for non-automated investments
- Performance tracking against appropriate benchmarks
- Documentation of investment theses for specific positions
- Expense tracking for all investment-related costs

For Janet, implementing these systems was as important as her actual investment selections. We helped her develop:

- Automated bi-weekly transfers from her checking account to investment accounts
- A written investment policy statement defining her strategy

- Quarterly portfolio review meetings with her advisor
- A curated reading list of investment books and resources
- A simple spreadsheet tracking her progress toward specific financial goals

These systems helped her maintain discipline through market volatility, reinforcing her new identity as an investor rather than just a saver.

The Family Investment Strategy

Building generational wealth requires looking beyond individual investment accounts to develop a coordinated family investment approach.

Cross-Generational Investment Planning

Consider these strategies for family-wide implementation:

1. **Family investment education:** Implement age-appropriate investment education for all family members, starting from childhood.
2. **Coordinated account structures:** Create a strategic architecture of account types across family members to maximize tax advantages and growth opportunities.
3. **Complementary investment allocations:** Consider how different family members' portfolios can work together rather than viewing each in isolation.
4. **Legacy investment planning:** Structure certain investments specifically for eventual transfer to the next generation in the most advantageous manner.

CHAPTER 6: AMPLIFY INVESTMENTS

5. **Family investment entities:** Consider family limited partnerships, LLCs, or other structures that facilitate collaborative investing while providing tax and asset protection advantages.
6. **Shared ownership strategies:** Implement partial ownership transfers of appreciating assets to younger generations over time to minimize transfer tax implications.

For the Thompson family we advised, implementing a family investment strategy transformed their approach to building wealth. Rather than each family member investing separately, they created a coordinated structure:

- Parents focused on income-producing investments aligned with their approaching retirement
- Adult children concentrated on maximum growth investments for their longer time horizon
- Family collaboration on direct real estate investments through a family LLC
- Strategic gifting of appreciating assets to minor children through UTMA accounts
- Regular family investment meetings where knowledge was shared and decisions discussed

"We've stopped thinking about 'my investments' and 'your investments,'" Mrs. Thompson explained. "Now we approach wealth building as a family system where each person plays a different but coordinated role."

Janet: Three Years Later

Let's revisit Janet's journey three years after implementing her investment strategy.

Her transformation has been remarkable:

Portfolio Development:

- Her initial $180,000 grew to approximately $245,000 despite some market volatility
- She continued adding $1,500 monthly from her income
- Her portfolio generated approximately $6,800 annually in dividends and interest
- She made her first direct real estate investment: a townhouse in a growing area

Knowledge Evolution:

- From being intimidated by investing, she developed confidence in her understanding
- She joined an investment club for continued education
- She began mentoring younger colleagues on investment basics
- She implemented advanced tax-loss harvesting during a market correction

Psychological Transformation:

- Her fear of loss evolved into a balanced understanding of risk and opportunity

CHAPTER 6: AMPLIFY INVESTMENTS

- Market fluctuations became viewed as normal rather than frightening
- She developed an investor identity rather than just a saver identity
- She began planning early retirement, now a viable option with her growing portfolio

"I wasted years playing it too safe," Janet reflected, "but instead of regret, I'm focused on the progress I've made and the opportunities ahead. Now I understand that my previous approach wasn't truly 'safe' at all—it was actually guaranteeing I'd fall short of my goals. Real safety comes from a diversified investment approach aligned with my time horizon."

Most importantly, Janet's relationship with money fundamentally changed. Rather than seeing money as something merely to be protected, she now views it as a tool to create opportunities and build wealth. This mindset shift—as much as the specific investments she made—transformed her financial trajectory.

Your Investment Amplification Journey

As we conclude this chapter, remember that transforming savings into strategically deployed investments is essential for building significant wealth. While saving creates the foundation, investing provides the growth engine that turns modest accumulation into substantial wealth over time.

Whether you're just beginning your investment journey like Janet was, or looking to optimize an existing portfolio, the principles in this chapter provide a framework for amplifying your wealth through strategic investing. Start where you are, implement one strategy at a time, and remain consistent in your approach.

For Black families building generational wealth, investment amplification takes on particular importance. Given historical barriers to wealth accumulation, we cannot afford the luxury of ultra-conservative approaches that fail to generate significant growth. Strategic, disciplined investing—while managing risk appropriately—provides the acceleration needed to close the wealth gap while creating new possibilities for current and future generations.

In the next chapter, we'll explore how to navigate life insurance as a wealth-building tool beyond just protection. But first, complete the action steps below to begin your investment amplification journey.

CHAPTER 6: AMPLIFY INVESTMENTS

ACTION STEP: Assess Your Current Investments and Identify Areas to Expand

- ☐ **Complete your investment inventory**
    - ☐ List all investment accounts and their current balances
    - ☐ Document the asset allocation within each account
    - ☐ Calculate your overall allocation across all accounts
    - ☐ Determine your current investment return over various time periods
    - ☐ Identify any investment concentrations or gaps
- ☐ **Define your investment goals and parameters**
    - ☐ Establish specific financial goals with amounts and time horizons
    - ☐ Determine your risk tolerance (both emotional and financial)
    - ☐ Define your desired income needs from investments
    - ☐ Identify your investment restrictions or preferences
    - ☐ Calculate required rate of return to meet your goals
- ☐ **Create your strategic asset allocation**
    - ☐ Determine your core portfolio allocation percentages
    - ☐ Identify strategic investments aligned with your specific goals
    - ☐ Select opportunistic categories appropriate for your situation
    - ☐ Create your target allocation across all investment categories
    - ☐ Develop your rebalancing strategy and triggers

- ☐ **Design your investment implementation system**
    - ☐ Select specific investment vehicles for each allocation category
    - ☐ Establish your automation strategy for contributions and investments
    - ☐ Create your investment calendar with review dates
    - ☐ Identify sources for ongoing education and research
    - ☐ Develop your record-keeping system
- ☐ **Identify strategic leverage opportunities (if appropriate)**
    - ☐ Assess potential credit sources available to you
    - ☐ Calculate potential returns with and without leverage
    - ☐ Establish risk management protocols for any leveraged investments
    - ☐ Determine appropriate leverage ratios for your situation
    - ☐ Create specific criteria for when leverage will be utilized

Remember: Investment success comes not from trying to pick winners or time markets, but from developing a strategic allocation aligned with your goals, implementing it systematically, and maintaining discipline through market cycles. Focus on the factors within your control—asset allocation, costs, tax efficiency, and consistent contributions—rather than attempting to predict short-term market movements.

CHAPTER 7

NAVIGATE A LIFE INSURANCE STRATEGY

"Life insurance isn't about the people who die. It's about the people who live."
—Unknown

"All I want is basic term life insurance," Thomas insisted during our initial consultation. "I don't need any of those expensive permanent policies that are just a waste of money."

Thomas, a 38-year-old software engineer with a wife and two young children, approached life insurance like many financially savvy professionals: with deep skepticism toward anything beyond low-cost term coverage. He had read numerous financial blogs and books advising that you should "buy term and invest the difference" rather than considering permanent life insurance.

"Life insurance should be simple," he continued. "I need coverage until my kids are grown and my investments are sufficient. A 20-year term policy for $1 million should cover it."

While Thomas's approach was perfectly reasonable for basic family protection, it overlooked a powerful dimension of life insurance that wealthy families have utilized for generations: its potential as a sophisticated wealth-building and wealth-transfer tool. This strategic dimension is why "Navigate a Life Insurance Strategy" is the seventh step in our Abundance Formula.

Beyond Basic Protection: Life Insurance as a Financial Instrument

For most Americans, life insurance serves a single purpose: providing financial protection for dependents in case of premature death. This basic function is indeed vital and should form the foundation of any life insurance strategy. However, viewing life insurance solely as a death benefit overlooks its potential as a versatile financial instrument with significant wealth-building capabilities.

The Protection-Only Perspective vs. Strategic Approach

The Protection-Only Perspective:

- Focuses exclusively on death benefit
- Views insurance as an expense rather than an asset
- Seeks lowest possible premium for required coverage
- Terminates coverage when dependents become self-sufficient
- Ignores additional features as "expensive add-ons"

CHAPTER 7: NAVIGATE A LIFE INSURANCE STRATEGY

The Strategic Approach:

- Recognizes both protection and living benefits
- Views certain insurance as a strategic asset class
- Optimizes multiple dimensions of policy design
- Maintains coverage as part of lifetime financial strategy
- Leverages additional features for specific financial objectives

While the protection-only perspective is appropriate for many situations, families building significant wealth benefit from understanding the full strategic potential of properly structured life insurance. This doesn't mean abandoning term insurance—rather, it means considering a more comprehensive strategy that may include both term and permanent coverage for different objectives.

The Multidimensional Value Proposition

Properly structured life insurance can provide multiple concurrent benefits:

1. **Income replacement and family protection** (the fundamental purpose)
2. **Tax-advantaged wealth accumulation** (with growth potentially free from income and capital gains taxes)
3. **Asset protection** (in many states, from creditors and legal judgments)
4. **Tax-free retirement income** (through policy loans and withdrawals)
5. **Long-term care funding** (through living benefit riders or conversion options)

6. **Estate tax liquidity** (providing cash to pay estate taxes without liquidating other assets)
7. **Business continuity** (funding buy-sell agreements and key person coverage)
8. **Wealth transfer efficiency** (passing assets to heirs with minimal tax impact)
9. **Charitable giving enhancement** (leveraging policies for philanthropic objectives)

While not every policy type offers all these advantages, understanding the full spectrum of possibilities allows you to design a comprehensive strategy aligned with your specific wealth-building goals.

Understanding Life Insurance Types: Beyond Term vs. Permanent

The conversation about life insurance is often reduced to a simple binary: term versus permanent. This oversimplification obscures the nuanced spectrum of policy types and their specific applications.

The Life Insurance Spectrum

Let's examine the major policy categories and their relative advantages:

Term Life Insurance

Key characteristics:

- Pure death benefit with no cash value accumulation

- Lower initial premiums compared to permanent coverage
- Coverage for specified period (typically 10-30 years)
- Renewable (usually at higher rates) or convertible to permanent policies
- Premium remains level throughout initial term

Strategic applications:

- Temporary protection needs (mortgage, children's dependency, specific debts)
- Maximum death benefit per premium dollar during high-need years
- Supplementing permanent coverage for specific periods of higher need
- Business protection for limited partnership or project durations
- Protecting specific financial obligations with defined timeframes

Whole Life Insurance

Key characteristics:

- Permanent coverage lasting lifetime (if premiums paid)
- Guaranteed cash value growth with minimum guaranteed returns
- Fixed premiums that do not increase
- Potential dividend payments (in participating policies)
- More conservative growth compared to other permanent types
- Strong contractual guarantees

Strategic applications:

- Core permanent death benefit needs
- Conservative cash value accumulation
- Estate planning and wealth transfer
- Predictable policy performance without variability
- Long-term care funding through conversion or riders
- Bank-alternative strategies (discussed later in this chapter)

Universal Life Insurance

Key characteristics:

- Permanent coverage with flexibility in premium payments and death benefits
- Unbundled policy structure (transparent insurance costs and cash value)
- Interest credited based on prevailing rates (with guaranteed minimums)
- Ability to increase or decrease coverage as needs change
- Less guarantees than whole life but potentially lower premiums

Strategic applications:

- Permanent coverage with premium flexibility
- Protection with potential for moderate cash accumulation
- Estate planning with ability to adjust death benefits
- Supplemental retirement funding with moderate risk tolerance
- Business continuation planning with adaptable coverage

Indexed Universal Life Insurance

Key characteristics:

- Universal life chassis with cash value growth linked to market indexes
- Downside protection (typically 0-1% floor on returns)
- Upside potential (typically capped at 8-14% depending on design)
- Similar flexibility to universal life in premiums and death benefits
- More growth potential than traditional universal life but with more variability

Strategic applications:

- Cash accumulation focus with upside potential and downside protection
- Supplemental retirement income through tax-free policy loans
- Business planning with growth potential for key person or buy-sell funding
- Estate planning with growth-oriented focus
- Living benefits through optional riders for chronic illness or long-term care

Variable Universal Life Insurance

Key characteristics:

- Universal life chassis with cash value invested in market-based sub-accounts
- Highest growth potential but also highest risk
- No downside protection beyond any optional riders
- Greatest flexibility in investment options
- Requires more active management and monitoring

Strategic applications:

- Maximum cash accumulation for investors with high risk tolerance
- Supplemental retirement planning with aggressive growth focus
- Estate planning for high-net-worth individuals with investment sophistication
- Business planning with growth focus for certain objectives
- Tax-advantaged investment vehicle when other options are maximized

Hybrid and Specialized Policies

Beyond these main categories, specialized policies combine features or address specific needs:

Long-term care/life insurance hybrids:

- Combine life insurance with long-term care benefits

- Allow access to death benefit for qualified long-term care expenses
- Eliminate "use it or lose it" concern of traditional long-term care insurance

Return of premium term:

- Term insurance that returns all premiums at the end of the term if no death claim
- Higher premiums than standard term but provides return of capital
- Bridge between traditional term and permanent products

Single premium policies:

- Funded with one large premium rather than ongoing payments
- Immediate cash value and potential tax advantages
- Useful for wealth transfer and estate planning

Understanding this spectrum allows for strategic selection of policy types aligned with specific objectives rather than limiting yourself to a binary term versus permanent decision.

Cash Value Life Insurance as a Wealth-Building Tool

While term insurance serves the essential protection function, properly structured cash value life insurance can serve as a powerful wealth-building tool with unique advantages unavailable in other financial vehicles.

The Unique Tax Treatment of Cash Value Life Insurance

Permanent life insurance receives preferential tax treatment that creates significant advantages:

1. **Tax-deferred growth:** Cash value grows without annual taxation on interest, dividends, or capital gains.
2. **Tax-free access to cash value:** When structured properly, policy loans and certain withdrawals can provide tax-free access to cash value.
3. **Income tax-free death benefit:** Proceeds paid to beneficiaries are generally free from income taxation.
4. **Potential estate tax advantages:** With proper ownership structure, policies can be excluded from the taxable estate.
5. **No contribution limits:** Unlike qualified retirement plans, there are no statutory limits on policy funding (though over-funding can create MEC status, discussed later).
6. **No required distributions:** Unlike IRAs and 401(k)s, there are no required minimum distributions during the policyholder's lifetime.
7. **No early withdrawal penalties:** Cash value can be accessed at any age without the penalties associated with qualified retirement plans.

This tax treatment creates a powerful financial tool when properly utilized as part of a comprehensive wealth-building strategy.

Policy Design: The Key to Effective Wealth Building

Not all permanent life insurance policies are created equal for wealth-building purposes. Strategic design makes the difference between mediocre and exceptional performance.

Key Design Elements for Wealth Building

1. **Minimized insurance costs:** Structuring the policy with the minimum death benefit required to maintain its tax advantages while maximizing cash value growth.
2. **Optimized premium-to-death-benefit ratio:** Finding the ideal balance between premium payments and death benefit to maximize cash value accumulation.
3. **Proper rider selection:** Adding only those riders that provide value aligned with specific objectives while avoiding unnecessary costs.
4. **Appropriate company selection:** Choosing insurance carriers based on financial strength, historical performance, and alignment with intended policy use.
5. **Strategic funding pattern:** Implementing a funding strategy that balances immediate cash value access, long-term growth, and policy sustainability.
6. **Modified Endowment Contract (MEC) avoidance:** Structuring funding to prevent the policy from becoming a MEC, which would eliminate some tax advantages.
7. **Policy owner/insured/beneficiary structure:** Establishing the appropriate legal relationships for optimal tax treatment and asset protection.

Maximum Funded, Minimum Death Benefit Design

For wealth-building purposes, a "maximum funded, minimum death benefit" design typically provides optimal results:

- Funding near the maximum allowed without creating MEC status
- Structuring with the lowest death benefit allowed by tax law for the premium
- Often utilizing a design with high initial premium and reduced ongoing payments
- Minimizing or eliminating unnecessary riders and features
- Selecting dividend options that maximize cash value growth (in participating policies)

This approach prioritizes cash value accumulation while maintaining the tax advantages and protection benefits of life insurance.

For Thomas, understanding these design principles shifted his perspective. After detailed analysis of his financial situation, we recommended a strategy that included both term insurance for maximum protection during his children's dependency years and a strategically designed whole life policy focused on wealth building and future flexibility.

"I never realized how much the specific design affects performance," Thomas acknowledged. "The illustrations showed dramatically different results with the same premium but different structures."

CHAPTER 7: NAVIGATE A LIFE INSURANCE STRATEGY

Life Insurance as Your Personal Banking System

One of the most powerful applications of cash value life insurance is the concept often called "Infinite Banking," "Bank On Yourself," or "Be Your Own Banker." This strategy uses specifically designed life insurance to create a personal banking system that provides financing for major purchases, investments, and opportunities.

The Personal Banking Concept

The core idea is relatively straightforward:

1. You establish properly structured cash value life insurance
2. The policy accumulates cash value over time
3. When you need capital, you borrow against your cash value rather than from traditional lenders
4. You repay the loan according to a schedule you determine
5. The repayments (with interest) go back into your policy, enhancing its growth

This approach creates several distinct advantages:

1. Recapture of Interest

When you finance purchases through traditional lenders, the interest you pay flows to the lending institution as profit. With the personal banking approach, you essentially pay interest to yourself, recapturing this typically lost capital.

Implementation strategy:

- Create a policy loan repayment schedule that includes principal plus an interest rate comparable to or higher than commercial rates
- Maintain disciplined repayment even though the policy doesn't require it
- Track the growth differential between policies used with this strategy versus those without it

2. Uninterrupted Compounding

One of the most powerful aspects of this strategy is that your cash value continues growing (in most policy designs) even while you have outstanding loans against it. This creates a form of "use it while you grow it" capability unavailable in most financial vehicles.

Implementation strategy:

- Select policy designs that continue to credit interest or dividends on the full cash value, even when loans are outstanding
- Understand the difference between direct recognition and non-direct recognition companies for this purpose
- Calculate the effective "arbitrage" between loan interest rates and ongoing cash value growth

3. Financing Flexibility

Unlike traditional loans with rigid requirements and schedules, policy loans offer remarkable flexibility:

- No credit checks or application process
- No predetermined repayment schedule
- Ability to customize repayment terms
- No prepayment penalties
- No impact on credit score

Implementation strategy:

- Establish clear personal guidelines for when policy loans will be utilized
- Create self-imposed repayment disciplines even though the policy doesn't require them
- Document specific objectives for each policy loan to maintain strategic focus

4. Death Benefit Net of Loans

If death occurs while policy loans are outstanding, the death benefit is paid minus the loan balance. This creates a form of automatic debt cancellation that protects your family or business from repayment obligations.

Implementation strategy:

- Maintain sufficient pure death benefit coverage beyond policies used for banking strategies

- Calculate the net death benefit considering outstanding loans when reviewing protection needs
- Consider additional term coverage if banking strategies reduce net death benefit below needed levels

Strategic Applications of Personal Banking

This approach can be used for numerous wealth-building purposes:

Major Purchases Financing

Instead of traditional financing for vehicles, equipment, or other major purchases, use policy loans with disciplined repayment.

Implementation example:

- For a $50,000 vehicle purchase, borrow against policy cash value
- Establish a 48-month repayment schedule at 6% interest
- Payments flow back into your policy rather than to a finance company
- At the end of the repayment period, your policy has grown by the principal plus interest

Investment Opportunity Funding

When investment opportunities arise, policy loans can provide quick, flexible capital.

Implementation example:

- Identify a real estate investment requiring $100,000 down payment
- Access funds via policy loan without liquidating other investments
- Use rental income to repay the policy loan plus interest
- Maintain ownership of both the growing policy and the new real estate investment

Business Capital Needs

Business owners can use this strategy for inventory, equipment, or expansion capital.

Implementation example:

- A business needs $75,000 for new equipment
- Rather than bank financing or depleting business cash reserves, use a policy loan
- Structure repayment from increased business revenue
- Business gains needed equipment while owner's policy continues growing

College Funding

Policy loans can provide flexible college funding while maintaining control and growth.

Implementation example:

- As college expenses arise, take policy loans rather than liquidating 529 plans during market downturns
- Repay loans during better market conditions
- Maintain flexibility for changing educational needs
- Preserve the policy's ongoing growth potential

For Melissa, a business owner we advised, implementing this strategy transformed both her personal finances and business operations. She established a properly designed whole life policy and funded it systematically over five years.

When an opportunity arose to purchase a competitor's business at a favorable price, she accessed $200,000 via policy loans rather than seeking bank financing with its accompanying application process, covenants, and fixed repayment schedule. She structured her own repayment plan aligned with the acquired business's cash flow projections.

"The flexibility was game-changing," Melissa explained. "I could move quickly to secure the deal, structure repayments around actual cash flow rather than bank requirements, and best of all, the interest I paid went back into my policy rather than to a bank."

Life Insurance in Estate Planning and Wealth Transfer

Beyond its living benefits, life insurance serves as a powerful tool for efficient wealth transfer and estate planning.

Estate Liquidity Provision

For estates potentially subject to estate taxes, life insurance can provide essential liquidity to pay these taxes without forcing the liquidation of other assets like businesses or real estate.

Implementation strategy:

- Calculate potential estate tax liability based on current net worth and growth projections
- Structure life insurance outside the taxable estate (typically through proper trust ownership)
- Ensure the policy face amount covers projected estate tax liability plus administrative costs
- Review and adjust coverage as net worth changes over time

Wealth Replacement Strategies

Life insurance can "replace" assets directed to non-family purposes, such as charitable giving or estate taxes.

Implementation example:

- A family donates a $1 million property to charity for tax benefits and philanthropic goals
- They use a portion of the tax savings to fund a life insurance policy
- The policy provides $1 million+ to heirs, "replacing" the donated property
- The family achieves both charitable and family legacy objectives

Equalization Among Heirs

When certain assets (like businesses or real estate) will pass to specific heirs, life insurance can provide equivalent value to other heirs.

Implementation example:

- A family business worth $2 million will pass to one child who works in the business
- A life insurance policy for $2 million names the other child as beneficiary
- Each child receives assets of equivalent value
- The business doesn't need to be sold or divided

Generation-Skipping Strategies

Life insurance can facilitate efficient multigenerational wealth transfer when properly structured.

Implementation strategy:

- Establish irrevocable life insurance trusts (ILITs) with appropriate generation-skipping provisions
- Fund the trust with gifts structured to minimize gift tax implications
- The trust owns policies on appropriate family members
- Policy proceeds benefit multiple generations with minimal transfer taxation

Dynasty Trust Funding

Specialized dynasty trusts can use life insurance to create multigenerational wealth protected from estate taxes at each generation.

Implementation strategy:

- Establish a dynasty trust in a jurisdiction with favorable trust laws
- The trust purchases life insurance on the grantor or other family members
- Trust assets, including insurance proceeds, can benefit multiple generations
- Proper structure can provide asset protection and tax advantages for generations

For the Williamson family we advised, life insurance solved a complex estate dilemma. Their $10 million family business would pass to their son who had worked in it for decades, but they wanted their daughter, who pursued a different career, to receive equivalent value. Through a strategically designed insurance policy owned by an irrevocable trust, they ensured their daughter would receive comparable assets while the business transferred intact to their son.

"We didn't want to force our son to buy out his sister, which might have required selling or borrowing against the business," Mr. Williamson explained. "The insurance solution gave us peace of mind that both children would be treated fairly without putting the business at risk."

Advanced Life Insurance Strategies

Beyond personal banking and basic estate planning, several advanced strategies leverage life insurance's unique characteristics for specific wealth-building objectives.

Premium Financing

This strategy involves borrowing money from a third party (typically a bank) to pay life insurance premiums, allowing for larger policies with minimal out-of-pocket costs.

Implementation considerations:

- Typically requires significant net worth (usually $5+ million)
- Involves using the policy (and sometimes other collateral) to secure the loan
- Creates arbitrage opportunity between loan interest rate and policy growth
- Requires careful monitoring of interest rates and policy performance
- Often used for estate planning with large coverage needs

Split-Dollar Arrangements

These arrangements divide policy costs and benefits between two parties, typically an employer and employee or family members.

CHAPTER 7: NAVIGATE A LIFE INSURANCE STRATEGY

Implementation examples:

- Economic benefit arrangement: One party pays for term costs while the other receives cash value benefits
- Loan regime arrangement: One party loans premium money to the other with specific repayment terms
- Private split-dollar: Family members share costs and benefits for estate planning purposes
- Each arrangement has specific tax implications requiring careful structuring

Deferred Compensation Funding

Life insurance can provide tax-advantaged funding for executive deferred compensation plans.

Implementation strategy:

- Company establishes nonqualified deferred compensation plan for key executives
- Corporate-owned life insurance funds the future obligation
- Policy cash value provides asset matching for the liability
- Death benefit protects company against loss of executive and provides tax-advantaged benefit funding

Charitable Planning with Life Insurance

Strategic use of life insurance can enhance philanthropic impact while creating tax advantages.

Implementation examples:

- Wealth replacement: Donate assets to charity while using insurance to replace value for heirs
- Charitable gift of policy: Donate an existing policy to a charity for current tax deduction
- Charity-owned insurance: Organization owns policy on donor with premiums gifted annually
- Each strategy creates unique combinations of tax benefits and charitable impact

Business Succession Funding

Life insurance provides ideal funding for business transition plans.

Implementation strategy:

- Structure buy-sell agreement defining transition upon specific events (death, disability, retirement)
- Use life insurance to fund purchase obligations created by the agreement
- Structure policy ownership appropriately for tax efficiency
- Review and update as business value changes

For Jackson, a successful entrepreneur approaching retirement, we implemented a combined strategy using life insurance to fund a business succession plan while creating tax-advantaged retirement income.

His company purchased a cash value policy on his life, which would provide the funding for a buy-sell agreement with his partners. Simultaneously, the policy's cash value growth created a tax-advantaged asset the company could later use to fund Jackson's deferred compensation plan, providing retirement income while creating business tax deductions.

"The dual purpose of the policy made it extraordinarily efficient," Jackson noted. "We solved the succession planning issue while simultaneously creating my retirement plan, with significant tax advantages for both."

Life Insurance Policy Selection and Management

Even with the right strategic approach, successful implementation depends on selecting appropriate policies and companies, then managing them effectively over time.

Life Insurance Company Selection Criteria

Not all insurance companies are equally suited for strategic wealth-building applications. Consider these factors:

1. Financial Strength and Stability

The long-term nature of life insurance requires confidence in the company's continued strength.

Evaluation approach:

- Review ratings from multiple independent agencies (A.M. Best, Moody's, S&P, Fitch)

- Consider longevity and history through various economic cycles
- Examine financial ratios beyond just ratings
- Review reinsurance arrangements and risk management practices

2. Product Design and Flexibility

Companies differ significantly in how their products are structured and the flexibility they offer.

Evaluation approach:

- Compare policy provisions for accessing cash value
- Evaluate cost of insurance structures and guarantees
- Review flexibility for premium payments and adjustments
- Assess rider availability and costs for desired features

3. Historical Performance

Past performance provides insight into company management and practices, though it doesn't guarantee future results.

Evaluation approach:

- For whole life, examine dividend history through various economic cycles
- For indexed products, review historical index crediting and cap rate adjustments

- For universal life, evaluate interest crediting history relative to prevailing rates
- Consider performance during both favorable and challenging economic periods

4. Direct vs. Non-Direct Recognition

For banking strategies, this distinction affects how policy loans impact dividend or interest crediting.

Evaluation approach:

- Understand whether loans reduce the dividend/interest on borrowed amounts (direct recognition) or not (non-direct)
- Evaluate the impact on banking strategy implementation
- Compare illustrated performance with varying loan utilization scenarios
- Consider the company's historical practices with loan interest rates

5. Policy Expenses and Transparency

Cost structure significantly impacts long-term performance.

Evaluation approach:

- Review mortality charges, expense loads, and surrender charges
- Assess transparency in how these costs are disclosed
- Compare cost indices among similar policies
- Consider the impact of costs on intended policy use

Policy Design Optimization

Beyond company selection, specific design elements must be optimized for intended use.

Protection-Focused Design

When death benefit is the primary objective:

- Emphasize guaranteed death benefit duration
- Consider guaranteed versus non-guaranteed designs
- Evaluate conversion options for term policies
- Structure premium schedules for long-term affordability

Cash Accumulation Design

When wealth building is the primary objective:

- Minimize death benefit relative to premium (while maintaining tax advantages)
- Front-load premiums when possible for earlier compounding
- Select appropriate dividend options for participating policies
- Consider paid-up additions riders to enhance early cash value

Banking Strategy Design

When personal banking is the primary objective:

- Select non-direct recognition companies when possible
- Structure for maximum early cash value

- Minimize surrender periods and charges
- Design for optimal policy loan provisions

Estate Planning Design

When wealth transfer is the primary objective:

- Focus on death benefit guarantees
- Structure ownership for estate tax exclusion
- Consider survivorship (second-to-die) designs for married couples
- Evaluate long-term premium funding requirements

Ongoing Policy Management

Life insurance is not a "set it and forget it" financial tool. Proper management includes:

1. **Annual policy reviews:** Assess performance against projections, company financial strength, and continued alignment with objectives.
2. **In-force illustrations:** Request updated projections based on current performance to identify any developing issues early.
3. **Strategic premium adjustments:** For flexible premium policies, adjust funding based on performance and changing objectives.
4. **Beneficiary reviews:** Regularly update beneficiary designations to reflect current intentions and circumstances.

5. **Ownership structure reviews:** Periodically assess whether policy ownership remains optimal for tax and estate planning.
6. **Conversion option evaluation:** For term policies, strategically assess conversion opportunities before they expire.
7. **Policy loan management:** For policies with outstanding loans, monitor loan balances relative to cash value and adjust as needed.
8. **1035 exchange consideration:** Evaluate whether policy exchange to newer, more efficient designs is appropriate as products evolve.

For Thomas, implementing these selection and management principles led to a coherent strategy incorporating:

- A 20-year term policy providing $1.5 million of family protection
- A strategically designed whole life policy for wealth building and flexibility
- Annual reviews coordinated with his overall financial planning
- A clear understanding of how each policy served different aspects of his financial strategy

"I initially saw life insurance as just an expense—a necessary one, but still just a cost," Thomas reflected. "Now I understand that properly structured permanent insurance is actually an asset class with unique characteristics that complement my other investments."

The Family Insurance Strategy

For families building generational wealth, a coordinated life insurance approach creates substantial advantages beyond individual policies.

Multi-Generational Insurance Planning

Strategic life insurance implementation across generations can create significant financial leverage.

Insuring Multiple Generations

Implementation strategy:

- Consider policies on children and grandchildren while premiums are lowest
- Implement juvenile insurance with ownership structures allowing future policy access
- Create systems for funding policies on younger generations through gifting strategies
- Coordinate with overall estate and wealth transfer planning

Policy Layering Across Family Members

Implementation strategy:

- Structure complementary coverage on different family members
- Consider survivorship policies for married couples when appropriate

- Implement policies serving different objectives for each family member
- Create coordination between business and personal coverage

Family Banking System Implementation

Implementation strategy:

- Establish policies specifically designed for family banking functions
- Create clear guidelines for when policy loans will be granted within the family
- Develop standardized family loan documentation and repayment expectations
- Coordinate with broader family governance structures

Family Insurance Education

Implementation strategy:

- Develop age-appropriate education about insurance concepts for all family members
- Create documentation explaining the strategic purpose of each family policy
- Include insurance understanding in broader financial literacy development
- Ensure multiple family members understand policy management requirements

CHAPTER 7: NAVIGATE A LIFE INSURANCE STRATEGY

For the Richardson family we advised, their multi-generational insurance strategy transformed how they approached both protection and wealth building. They established:

- Traditional protection policies on both parents
- Strategically designed whole life policies for their banking system
- Small permanent policies on each child, with carefully structured ownership
- A survivorship policy owned by a trust for eventual estate liquidity
- Annual family meetings including discussion of their insurance strategy
- Clear documentation for future generations about policy management

"We've created an insurance ecosystem rather than just a collection of policies," Mr. Richardson explained. "Each policy serves a specific purpose in our family wealth strategy, with benefits that extend across generations."

Thomas: Four Years Later

Let's revisit Thomas's journey four years after implementing his comprehensive life insurance strategy.

His transformation has been remarkable:

Strategic Coverage Implementation:

- Maintained his 20-year term policy for core family protection

- Fully funded his strategically designed whole life policy
- Added a small policy on his wife for family banking purposes
- Established juvenile policies for both children

Banking Strategy Utilization:

- Used policy loans to purchase a family vehicle, repaying himself rather than a finance company
- Accessed funds for a timely investment opportunity during a market correction
- Created his own "financing system" for major purchases and investments
- Recaptured thousands in interest that would have gone to traditional lenders

Knowledge Evolution:

- From being skeptical of anything beyond term insurance, he developed sophisticated understanding of insurance as a financial tool
- He began educating friends and colleagues about strategic insurance uses
- He implemented regular policy reviews coordinated with his overall financial planning
- He developed specific plans for policy optimization at various life stages

CHAPTER 7: NAVIGATE A LIFE INSURANCE STRATEGY

Financial Position Improvement:

- His whole life policy accumulated cash value exceeding premiums paid
- He created tax diversification in his overall financial picture
- He established the foundation for significant tax-free retirement income
- He developed enhanced financial flexibility through readily accessible policy cash value

"I'm embarrassed by how dismissive I was initially," Thomas reflected. "I almost missed out on a powerful financial tool because I had absorbed the overly simplistic 'buy term and invest the difference' mantra without understanding the nuances. Now life insurance is a cornerstone of our family's wealth-building strategy."

Most importantly, Thomas's relationship with life insurance fundamentally changed. Rather than viewing it merely as an expense for protection, he now understands it as a multi-dimensional financial tool that creates unique advantages unavailable in other financial vehicles.

Your Life Insurance Strategy Journey

As we conclude this chapter, remember that navigating life insurance strategically involves looking beyond the basic protection function to understand its potential as a sophisticated wealth-building and wealth-transfer tool.

Whether you currently have only basic coverage like Thomas initially did, or are looking to optimize an existing insurance portfolio, the principles in this chapter provide a framework for leveraging life insurance's unique characteristics. Start where you are, implement one strategy at a time, and coordinate your insurance approach with your overall wealth-building plan.

For Black families building generational wealth, strategic life insurance implementation creates particularly significant advantages. The tax treatment, asset protection, and wealth transfer efficiency of properly structured policies can help accelerate wealth building while creating financial stability that extends across generations.

In the next chapter, we'll explore how to create a comprehensive tax wealth strategy that keeps more of your hard-earned money working for you instead of flowing to the government. But first, complete the action steps below to begin optimizing your life insurance approach.

ACTION STEP: Review and Update Your Life Insurance Policies

- **Complete your insurance inventory**
    - List all existing policies with type, death benefit, and premium
    - Document cash values for any permanent policies
    - Identify policy owners, insureds, and beneficiaries
    - Determine if any term conversion options exist and their deadlines
    - Calculate your total current coverage across all policies

CHAPTER 7: NAVIGATE A LIFE INSURANCE STRATEGY

- [ ] **Assess your insurance needs**
  - [ ] Calculate your basic protection requirement (income replacement, debt payoff, education funding, etc.)
  - [ ] Identify specific business needs (key person, buy-sell funding, etc.)
  - [ ] Determine wealth-building objectives that insurance might address
  - [ ] Evaluate estate planning considerations requiring insurance
- [ ] **Evaluate your current coverage gaps**
  - [ ] Compare your needs assessment against your current coverage
  - [ ] Identify any protection shortfalls requiring immediate attention
  - [ ] Determine if your current policies serve wealth-building objectives
  - [ ] Assess whether your coverage addresses estate planning concerns
  - [ ] Identify policies that may no longer serve their original purpose
- [ ] **Develop your strategic insurance plan**
  - [ ] Define specific roles for each type of insurance in your financial strategy
  - [ ] Determine appropriate balance between term and permanent coverage
  - [ ] Identify potential applications for banking strategies if appropriate
  - [ ] Create coordination between personal and business coverage

- [ ] Establish clear objectives for any new or restructured policies
- [ ] **Implement your insurance management system**
    - [ ] Schedule annual policy reviews with specific evaluation criteria
    - [ ] Create a system for tracking policy performance against projections
    - [ ] Document intended purpose and management guidelines for each policy
    - [ ] Establish policy loan guidelines if implementing banking strategies
    - [ ] Coordinate insurance reviews with overall financial planning

---

Remember: Life insurance can be much more than just protection against premature death. When properly structured, it represents a unique asset class with tax, legal, and financial characteristics unavailable in any other financial vehicle. The key is intentional design aligned with your specific wealth-building objectives.

CHAPTER 8

CREATE A TAX WEALTH STRATEGY

"It's not how much you make, but how much you keep that matters."
—Robert Kiyosaki

"**I** got a big raise last year, but somehow I feel like I'm taking home less money."

This common complaint came from Elijah, a 42-year-old marketing executive who had recently been promoted to a senior leadership position. His salary had increased from $110,000 to $165,000, but after moving into a higher tax bracket and losing certain deductions, his financial progress didn't match his career advancement.

"I'm working harder, have more responsibility, and am earning more on paper," he explained during our first meeting. "But after taxes take their bite, I'm barely ahead of where I was before. It feels like I'm on a financial treadmill—running faster but not getting further ahead."

Elijah's frustration highlights a reality that many successful professionals discover as their income grows: without strategic tax planning, a significant portion of your increasing wealth can be lost to taxation. This drain on wealth-building potential is why "Create a Tax Wealth Strategy" is the eighth step in our Abundance Formula.

Beyond Tax Preparation: The Tax Strategy Mindset

Most Americans approach taxes reactively—gathering documents in February or March, preparing returns (or having them prepared) to calculate what they owe, and then repeating the process the following year. This approach treats taxation as an inevitable outcome rather than a variable that can be strategically influenced.

The Tax Preparation vs. Tax Strategy Paradigm

The difference between these approaches is profound:

Tax Preparation (Reactive):

- Focuses on accurate reporting of past transactions
- Operates on an annual cycle
- Aims to avoid penalties and interest
- Emphasizes compliance with tax laws
- Primarily backward-looking
- Accepts tax outcomes as given

Tax Strategy (Proactive):

- Focuses on structuring future transactions for optimal tax outcomes

- Operates continuously throughout the year
- Aims to legally minimize tax obligations
- Emphasizes planning within tax law frameworks
- Primarily forward-looking
- Views tax outcomes as variables to be managed

This shift from reactive tax preparation to proactive tax strategy represents one of the most significant opportunities for wealth acceleration available to successful individuals and families.

The Wealth Impact of Strategic Tax Planning

The cumulative impact of effective tax strategy is often underestimated. Consider that:

1. **Tax savings are immediate and guaranteed.** Unlike investment returns which are variable and future-oriented, every dollar saved in taxes is an immediate, guaranteed 100% return on the effort invested in tax planning.
2. **Tax savings compound over time.** When reinvested, dollars saved through tax strategy grow and compound, multiplying the benefit beyond the initial savings.
3. **Tax strategy is cumulative.** Many tax planning techniques, once implemented, continue generating benefits year after year with minimal additional effort.
4. **Tax strategy is largely within your control.** Unlike market performance or interest rates, tax outcomes can be significantly influenced by your own decisions and structures.

For a professional like Elijah at a marginal tax rate of 35% (federal plus state), every $1,000 of income subject to tax costs $350. Over a 30-year career, reducing taxable income by just $20,000 annually would save $210,000 in taxes. If those savings were invested at 8% annually, they would grow to approximately $2.5 million—potentially the difference between comfortable and luxurious retirement.

Understanding the Tax Code: Rules vs. Tools

Many people view tax laws as a complex set of rules to be followed. The wealthy and financially sophisticated, however, recognize that the tax code is actually a set of tools that, when properly utilized, can significantly enhance wealth building.

The Strategic Perspective on Taxation

The tax code doesn't simply extract revenue—it also incentivizes specific behaviors and economic activities. By aligning your financial activities with these incentivized behaviors, you can legally reduce your tax burden while building wealth more efficiently.

Key areas where the tax code provides strategic opportunities include:

1. **Business ownership:** Numerous advantages for entrepreneurs and business owners
2. **Real estate investment:** Significant benefits for property investors
3. **Retirement saving:** Tax-advantaged accounts and strategies
4. **Charitable giving:** Incentives for philanthropy

5. **Family wealth transfer:** Structured approaches to intergenerational transfers
6. **Investment management:** Strategies for tax-efficient investing
7. **Healthcare financing:** Tax-advantaged approaches to medical expenses

In each of these areas, the tax code contains provisions that can be leveraged as wealth-building tools rather than merely followed as compliance requirements.

The Legitimate Tax Avoidance Mindset

It's essential to distinguish between tax evasion (illegal non-payment of taxes) and tax avoidance (legal reduction of tax liability). As Judge Learned Hand famously wrote:

"Anyone may arrange his affairs so that his taxes shall be as low as possible; he is not bound to choose that pattern which best pays the treasury. There is not even a patriotic duty to increase one's taxes. Over and over again the Courts have said that there is nothing sinister in so arranging affairs as to keep taxes as low as possible. Everyone does it, rich and poor alike and all do right, for nobody owes any public duty to pay more than the law demands."

Ethical tax strategy involves:

- Complete and accurate reporting of all legally required information
- Claiming all deductions and credits to which you're legitimately entitled
- Structuring transactions and entities in tax-advantaged ways

- Timing income and deductions strategically
- Utilizing the tax code as it was designed—as a set of rules with specific incentives

This approach represents responsible financial stewardship rather than attempting to "game the system" or evade legitimate obligations.

Business Structures and Tax Benefits

For many wealth builders, business ownership provides the single most powerful set of tax advantages available. The specific legal structure of your business significantly impacts these advantages.

Key Business Entity Options

Different business structures offer varying tax treatments and benefits:

Sole Proprietorship

Tax characteristics:

- Pass-through taxation (business income reported on personal return)
- Subject to self-employment tax on all profits (15.3% on first $142,800 in 2021, 2.9% Medicare tax on all earnings)
- Business losses directly deductible against other income (subject to limitations)
- Minimal formation and compliance requirements

Strategic applications:

- Starting businesses with minimal initial profits
- Simplified structure for side businesses
- Testing business concepts before formal entity formation
- Single-member service businesses with straightforward operations

Limited Liability Company (LLC)

Tax characteristics:

- Flexible taxation (can elect different tax treatments)
- Default treatment: Single-member LLC taxed as sole proprietorship, multi-member as partnership
- Can elect S-Corporation or C-Corporation treatment
- State law liability protection with federal tax flexibility

Strategic applications:

- Real estate investments requiring liability protection
- Businesses seeking operational flexibility
- Holding companies for various assets
- Multi-owner businesses requiring customized profit distributions

S-Corporation

Tax characteristics:

- Pass-through taxation (income flows to personal returns)
- Distributions above reasonable salary not subject to self-employment tax
- Limited to 100 shareholders, U.S. citizens/residents only
- Single class of stock requirement
- More rigid operational requirements than LLCs

Strategic applications:

- Service businesses with significant profit
- Businesses where owner actively works in the operation
- Situations where self-employment tax reduction is primary goal
- Businesses with straightforward ownership structures

C-Corporation

Tax characteristics:

- Separate taxpaying entity (corporate tax rates apply)
- Potential for double taxation (corporate level and dividend level)
- Broader range of deductible benefits for owner-employees
- Unlimited shareholders and ownership structures
- Ability to retain earnings for growth at corporate rates

Strategic applications:

- Businesses planning to reinvest significant profits for growth
- Companies seeking outside investment or planning public offering
- Situations where corporate-level deductions exceed double-tax cost
- International business operations
- Businesses where accumulated earnings concerns can be addressed

Partnership

Tax characteristics:

- Pass-through taxation with significant flexibility
- Special allocations of profit and loss allowed
- Various classes of ownership possible
- Complex compliance requirements
- Self-employment tax treatment varies by partnership type and participation

Strategic applications:

- Businesses with complex ownership or profit-sharing arrangements
- Professional service firms with multiple owners
- Investment vehicles with diverse investor classes
- Joint ventures between existing businesses or entities

Strategic Tax Planning Through Business Structures

Beyond basic entity selection, several advanced strategies leverage business structures for tax advantages:

1. Multiple Entity Strategies

Using complementary business structures can optimize overall taxation.

Implementation examples:

- Management company (S-Corporation) providing services to operating company
- Holding company owning intellectual property and leasing to operating business
- Real estate entity leasing property to business operation
- Family limited partnership owning business real estate

These arrangements, when properly structured with legitimate business purpose and appropriate transfer pricing, can create significant tax efficiencies while managing liability.

2. Qualified Business Income Deduction Optimization

The Tax Cuts and Jobs Act created the Section 199A deduction, allowing up to 20% of qualified business income to be deducted by pass-through business owners.

Implementation strategy:

- Structure business operations to maximize qualifying income

- Manage taxable income thresholds to avoid phase-outs
- Consider entity structures that optimize this deduction
- Evaluate reasonable compensation strategies for S-Corporation owners
- Assess segregating qualified vs. non-qualified business activities

3. Retirement Plan Strategies Through Business Ownership

Business ownership enables access to expanded retirement plan options beyond those available to employees.

Implementation strategy:

- Evaluate Solo 401(k), SEP-IRA, and SIMPLE IRA options for smaller businesses
- Consider defined benefit plans for high-income business owners
- Implement cash balance plans for maximum tax-deferred contributions
- Structure compensation to optimize plan contributions
- Coordinate business retirement plans with personal retirement strategies

4. Family Employment Strategies

Employing family members can create legitimate tax advantages when properly structured.

Implementation strategy:

- Hire children for appropriate roles (shifting income to lower brackets)
- Employ spouse to enable additional benefit and retirement plan options
- Document legitimate work performed and pay reasonable compensation
- Implement appropriate payroll and tax compliance
- Consider educational benefits and training opportunities

For Elijah, business structure created transformative tax advantages. After our analysis, he established an S-Corporation for his growing consulting practice (which he had previously operated as a sole proprietorship alongside his employment). By paying himself a reasonable salary and taking the remaining profit as distributions, he significantly reduced his self-employment tax burden while creating additional deduction opportunities.

"The business structure alone saved me over $12,000 in taxes the first year," Elijah noted. "And it created a framework for even more strategic tax planning as my consulting practice grew."

Real Estate and Tax Advantages

Real estate investment offers some of the most powerful tax benefits available—one reason it features prominently in the portfolios of tax-sophisticated wealth builders.

Core Real Estate Tax Benefits

Several key advantages make real estate particularly tax-efficient:

1. Depreciation

This non-cash deduction allows investors to write off the cost of buildings over time (27.5 years for residential, 39 years for commercial), creating tax losses even while the property generates positive cash flow.

Implementation strategy:

- Allocate as much purchase price as legitimately possible to depreciable improvements rather than non-depreciable land
- Consider cost segregation studies to accelerate depreciation for certain components
- Understand recapture provisions upon sale and strategies to minimize recapture
- Coordinate depreciation strategies with overall income and loss position

2. Mortgage Interest Deduction

Interest on loans for investment properties is generally fully deductible against property income.

Implementation strategy:

- Structure financing to maximize deductible interest

- Consider interest-only periods to maximize deduction in early years
- Evaluate refinancing strategies for optimal tax treatment
- Understand and comply with limitations on business interest deductions

3. Operating Expense Deductions

Ordinary and necessary expenses for managing, conserving, or maintaining rental property are deductible when incurred.

Implementation strategy:

- Implement systems to track and document all deductible expenses
- Understand which expenses must be capitalized versus immediately deducted
- Consider timing of expenses for optimal tax effect
- Evaluate service provider relationships for maximum deductibility

4. Capital Gains Treatment on Appreciation

When investment property is sold, appreciation is typically taxed at favorable long-term capital gains rates rather than ordinary income rates.

Implementation strategy:

- Hold properties for at least one year and a day to qualify for long-term gains rates

- Consider timing of sales to manage overall tax picture
- Evaluate installment sale treatment for larger dispositions
- Coordinate gains with available losses or other deductions

5. 1031 Exchanges

This powerful provision allows deferral of capital gains taxes when one investment property is exchanged for another "like-kind" property.

Implementation strategy:

- Understand strict timeline requirements (45 days to identify, 180 days to close)
- Work with qualified intermediaries to ensure proper exchange structure
- Consider reverse exchanges when appropriate for timing reasons
- Evaluate partial exchanges when full replacement isn't desired
- Understand boot recognition and mortgage replacement requirements

Advanced Real Estate Tax Strategies

Beyond these core benefits, several advanced strategies can further enhance real estate's tax advantages:

1. Real Estate Professional Status

For those qualifying as real estate professionals, rental real estate losses can offset other income, including W-2 wages, without limitation.

Implementation strategy:

- Document 750+ hours and more than half of all professional time spent in real estate activities
- Maintain contemporaneous time logs to support the designation
- Consider having one spouse qualify while the other maintains employment
- Evaluate grouping elections for properties to maximize the benefit
- Structure business entities to support professional status documentation

2. Short-Term Rental Strategies

Properties rented for average periods of 7 days or less may qualify for both depreciation benefits and avoidance of passive activity loss limitations.

CHAPTER 8: CREATE A TAX WEALTH STRATEGY

Implementation strategy:

- Structure ownership to qualify for maximum tax benefits
- Document material participation to avoid passive activity treatment
- Understand local regulations regarding short-term rentals
- Consider hybrid approaches with both short and longer-term rentals
- Evaluate business entity structure for optimal tax treatment

3. Opportunity Zone Investments

The Tax Cuts and Jobs Act created Opportunity Zones, offering significant tax benefits for investing capital gains in designated economic development areas.

Implementation strategy:

- Identify qualifying capital gains for potential deferral
- Understand the strict 180-day timeline for investment
- Evaluate qualified opportunity funds based on investment quality and tax benefits
- Consider the 10-year holding period required for maximum tax advantage
- Coordinate opportunity zone investments with overall portfolio strategy

4. Cost Segregation

This engineering-based study identifies components of real property that can be depreciated on accelerated schedules (5, 7, or 15 years instead of 27.5 or 39 years).

Implementation strategy:

- Consider for properties with purchase price exceeding $500,000
- Evaluate cost-benefit analysis based on anticipated holding period
- Understand impact on eventual sale and depreciation recapture
- Coordinate with bonus depreciation opportunities when available
- Consider timing of studies for optimal tax impact

5. Self-Directed IRA for Real Estate

Using self-directed IRAs to hold real estate can create tax-deferred or tax-free growth depending on the account type.

Implementation strategy:

- Work with specialized custodians offering real estate IRA options
- Understand prohibited transaction rules regarding personal use
- Evaluate debt-financing limitations and UBIT implications
- Consider Roth conversion strategies for tax-free growth
- Implement appropriate entity structures for liability management

For Marcus, a physician we advised, implementing real estate tax strategies transformed his financial trajectory. He qualified as a real estate professional (through his spouse's activities) while building a portfolio of residential rental properties. The resulting tax losses offset a significant portion of his high-bracket medical income while the properties continued appreciating and generating positive cash flow.

"I went from paying nearly 40% of my income in taxes to less than 20%," Marcus shared. "Meanwhile, my real estate portfolio has more than doubled in value over five years. The tax strategies not only saved me money but accelerated my ability to acquire more properties."

Trust Strategies for Tax Efficiency

Trusts represent some of the most powerful tools for tax optimization, asset protection, and efficient wealth transfer. While often associated primarily with estate planning, certain trust structures offer significant income tax benefits as well.

Key Trust Types for Tax Planning

Various trust structures serve different tax planning objectives:

1. Intentionally Defective Grantor Trusts (IDGTs)

These trusts create a separation between income tax treatment and estate tax treatment, with the grantor paying income taxes on trust assets while removing them from the taxable estate.

Implementation strategy:

- Transfer appreciating assets expected to grow significantly
- Structure sales to the trust using installment notes
- Implement specific grantor trust provisions
- Consider for business interests or investment assets
- Coordinate with overall estate freeze strategies

2. Charitable Remainder Trusts (CRTs)

These split-interest trusts provide income to non-charitable beneficiaries for a period, with remaining assets going to charity, creating current tax deductions and capital gains management.

Implementation strategy:

- Fund with highly appreciated assets to avoid immediate capital gains
- Select appropriate payout structure (annuity vs. unitrust)
- Determine optimal term (lifetime or fixed period)
- Consider "wealth replacement" with life insurance for heirs
- Coordinate charitable objectives with tax planning

3. Spousal Lifetime Access Trusts (SLATs)

These irrevocable trusts benefit a spouse during their lifetime while removing assets from the taxable estate, potentially maintaining indirect access while achieving tax benefits.

CHAPTER 8: CREATE A TAX WEALTH STRATEGY

Implementation strategy:

- Fund with assets up to lifetime gift tax exemption amount
- Structure with different terms if creating reciprocal trusts
- Include flexibility provisions for changing circumstances
- Consider life insurance funding within the trust
- Coordinate with other estate planning vehicles

4. Incomplete Non-Grantor Trusts (INGs)

These trusts can shift income taxation to lower-tax or no-tax states while maintaining some grantor control.

Implementation strategy:

- Establish in favorable jurisdictions (Delaware, Nevada, etc.)
- Transfer income-producing assets with state tax impact
- Structure distribution committees appropriately
- Maintain incomplete gift status for transfer tax purposes
- Coordinate with overall multi-state tax planning

5. Qualified Personal Residence Trusts (QPRTs)

These trusts allow transfer of a residence at a discounted gift tax value while retaining the right to live in the home for a specified term.

Implementation strategy:

- Select appropriate term based on life expectancy and objectives
- Understand continued obligation for property expenses

- Consider multiple QPRTs for different property interests
- Coordinate with overall estate plan and housing needs
- Evaluate rental arrangements after term expiration

Strategic Trust Implementation

Beyond selecting appropriate trust types, several implementation considerations maximize tax benefits:

1. Jurisdictional Selection

Different states offer varying trust laws and tax treatments, creating planning opportunities.

Implementation strategy:

- Evaluate state income taxation of trusts for non-grantor trusts
- Consider asset protection features of different jurisdictions
- Assess decanting provisions for future flexibility
- Evaluate dynasty trust potential and rule against perpetuities
- Consider trustee requirements and availability in various jurisdictions

2. Timing Strategies

Strategic timing of trust formation and funding can significantly impact tax outcomes.

CHAPTER 8: CREATE A TAX WEALTH STRATEGY

Implementation strategy:

- Coordinate with market conditions for optimal valuation
- Consider interest rate environments for certain techniques
- Align with business transaction timing when relevant
- Evaluate anticipated tax law changes
- Implement based on personal income fluctuations when beneficial

3. Grantor vs. Non-Grantor Status Management

The income tax treatment of trusts significantly impacts their benefits.

Implementation strategy:

- Select grantor status for appreciating assets to maximize growth
- Consider non-grantor status for income-producing assets in high-tax situations
- Evaluate "toggling" provisions to change status if beneficial
- Understand situations where blended approaches work best
- Coordinate trust income tax status with overall tax planning

4. Generation-Skipping Planning

Strategic use of the generation-skipping transfer tax exemption can create multi-generational tax benefits.

Implementation strategy:

- Allocate exemption to trusts with highest growth potential

- Consider late allocation strategies when appropriate
- Implement dynasty trust provisions in favorable jurisdictions
- Coordinate with lifetime gifting strategies
- Leverage insurance for exemption leveraging when appropriate

For the Williamson family we advised, trust strategies created both immediate tax benefits and long-term wealth preservation. They implemented an intentionally defective grantor trust to hold their growing business interests. This structure allowed them to:

- Remove the business appreciation from their taxable estate
- Continue paying income taxes on business profits (effectively tax-free gifts to the trust)
- Maintain operational control through carefully structured provisions
- Create multi-generational wealth transfer with minimal tax impact
- Protect business assets from potential creditors or claims

"The trust strategy not only reduced our eventual estate tax but actually accelerated the growth of assets for our children and grandchildren," Mr. Williamson explained. "By paying the income taxes personally, we're essentially making additional tax-free transfers every year while maintaining the flexibility we need."

CHAPTER 8: CREATE A TAX WEALTH STRATEGY

Combining "Buy, Borrow, Die" with Strategic Tax Planning

As introduced in earlier chapters, the "Buy, Borrow, Die" strategy represents a powerful approach used by wealthy families to preserve and grow assets while maintaining liquidity and minimizing taxes. When integrated with comprehensive tax planning, this strategy becomes even more effective.

Key Tax Optimization Elements

Several specific tax planning techniques enhance the "Buy, Borrow, Die" approach:

1. Strategic Asset Location

Determining which assets to hold in which types of accounts or entities significantly impacts tax efficiency.

Implementation strategy:

- Hold appreciating assets likely to be held until death in taxable accounts (for basis step-up)
- Place income-producing assets in tax-advantaged accounts where possible
- Consider entity structures for assets with specific tax advantages (real estate, businesses)
- Evaluate trust ownership for assets with appreciation or income-shifting potential

- Implement family limited partnerships or LLCs for certain assets

2. Tax-Efficient Borrowing Structures

The "borrow" component can be optimized through strategic loan structuring.

Implementation strategy:

- Evaluate potential tax deductibility of different borrowing approaches
- Consider business entity borrowing versus personal when appropriate
- Implement strategies that avoid triggering taxable events
- Structure loans to maximize legitimate interest deductions
- Coordinate borrowing with overall entity planning

3. Basis Management Strategies

Managing cost basis during life and at death significantly impacts eventual taxation.

Implementation strategy:

- Identify high-basis assets for lifetime gifting
- Retain low-basis assets for step-up at death
- Implement strategic harvesting of losses to offset gains
- Consider partial interest discounting techniques
- Evaluate community property advantages for married couples

4. Charitable Integration

Incorporating charitable planning can enhance overall tax efficiency.

Implementation strategy:

- Donate appreciated assets rather than cash when possible
- Consider charitable remainder trusts for appreciated assets
- Evaluate donor-advised funds for timing flexibility
- Implement qualified charitable distributions from IRAs when eligible
- Coordinate charitable planning with income management strategies

5. Lifetime Exemption Utilization

Strategic use of lifetime gift tax exemptions enhances overall efficiency.

Implementation strategy:

- Prioritize assets with highest appreciation potential for exemption use
- Consider valuation discount opportunities for partial interests
- Implement grantor trust strategies to enhance exemption efficiency
- Evaluate generation-skipping allocation for multi-generational planning
- Coordinate with overall asset protection objectives

For Richard, a successful business owner approaching retirement, integrating "Buy, Borrow, Die" with comprehensive tax planning created remarkable results. He implemented a strategy that included:

- Retaining low-basis business interests for eventual step-up
- Establishing lines of credit against business and investment assets
- Creating non-grantor trusts in low-tax jurisdictions for certain income streams
- Implementing strategic charitable giving using appreciated securities
- Structuring his estate plan to maximize basis step-up opportunities

"The integrated approach changed everything," Richard noted. "Instead of selling assets and paying capital gains tax, I'm borrowing against them when needed. Instead of creating taxable income, I'm generating tax-free liquidity. And my estate plan ensures minimal taxation when these assets eventually pass to my heirs."

Personal Tax Optimization Strategies

While business, real estate, and trust strategies offer powerful tax advantages, numerous personal tax optimization approaches can be implemented regardless of business ownership or investment strategy.

Income Timing and Characterization

Strategic timing and characterization of income can significantly impact taxation.

1. Income Timing Strategies

Implementation approaches:

- Accelerate or defer income between tax years based on anticipated brackets
- Bunch itemized deductions into alternate years
- Consider Roth conversion strategies during lower-income years
- Time capital gains recognition based on other income and available losses
- Implement installment sales for controlled income recognition

2. Income Characterization Strategies

Implementation approaches:

- Structure compensation packages to optimize between ordinary income and capital gains
- Evaluate equity-based compensation options (RSUs, options, etc.)
- Consider carried interest structures when appropriate
- Implement strategies to convert ordinary income to capital gains when possible
- Evaluate qualified business income characterization opportunities

Retirement Accounts and Benefits Optimization

Retirement accounts offer significant tax advantages beyond basic contributions.

1. Strategic Account Selection

Implementation approaches:

- Balance pre-tax (traditional) and post-tax (Roth) contributions
- Consider backdoor Roth strategies for high-income earners
- Evaluate mega-backdoor Roth approaches through employer plans
- Implement HSA accounts as stealth retirement accounts
- Coordinate spousal retirement strategies

2. Withdrawal and Distribution Planning

Implementation approaches:

- Develop multi-year tax projection for retirement distributions
- Implement strategic Roth conversions in lower-income years
- Consider qualified charitable distributions for required minimum distributions
- Evaluate Net Unrealized Appreciation strategies for employer stock
- Implement strategic inheritance planning for retirement accounts

Family Tax Planning

Integrating family members into tax planning creates additional opportunities.

1. Income Shifting Strategies

Implementation approaches:

- Employ children in family businesses (legitimate roles with appropriate documentation)
- Consider family management companies for centralized services
- Implement family limited partnerships for investment assets
- Evaluate UTMA/UGMA accounts for appropriate assets
- Structure gifts to maximize tax efficiency

2. Education Planning Strategies

Implementation approaches:

- Implement 529 plans with strategic ownership structure
- Consider Coverdell accounts for specific education needs
- Evaluate tax credits versus deductions for education expenses
- Implement education business deductions when applicable
- Structure educational assistance through business entities when possible

Healthcare Tax Strategies

Healthcare costs offer several tax planning opportunities.

Implementation approaches:

- Maximize HSA contributions and investments
- Implement premium conversion through employer cafeteria plans
- Structure medical expense reimbursement through business entities
- Evaluate medical expense timing to maximize itemized deductions
- Consider health insurance premium deductions for self-employed individuals

State and Local Tax Planning

With state income tax rates reaching 13% in some jurisdictions, state tax planning is increasingly important.

Implementation approaches:

- Evaluate domicile planning for those with flexibility
- Implement trust strategies to shift income to lower-tax jurisdictions
- Consider business entity structures that minimize state tax exposure
- Time transactions based on residence planning
- Leverage state tax credits and incentives programs

For Elijah, implementing personal tax optimization strategies alongside his business planning created substantial benefits. His comprehensive approach included:

- Maximizing retirement contributions through his S-Corporation
- Implementing a timing strategy that balanced salary and distributions
- Establishing an HSA with investment options
- Strategically bunching charitable contributions in alternate years
- Employing his college-age son in legitimate marketing roles

"The combined strategies reduced my effective tax rate by almost 15 percentage points," Elijah shared. "That's money that's now building wealth instead of going to taxes."

Tax Planning for Different Financial Phases

Tax strategy must evolve through different phases of wealth building, with approaches tailored to each stage.

Accumulation Phase Tax Strategy

During primary wealth-building years, focus on strategies that maximize after-tax investment while creating long-term advantages.

Key strategies:

- Maximize tax-advantaged retirement contributions

- Implement business structures that reduce self-employment taxes
- Establish foundation for real estate tax advantages
- Begin basis management for investment assets
- Implement family income-shifting where appropriate
- Establish framework for eventual wealth transfer planning

Peak Earning Phase Tax Strategy

When income reaches its highest levels, focus on strategies that minimize current taxation while establishing future flexibility.

Key strategies:

- Implement advanced retirement strategies beyond basic contributions
- Establish strategic borrowing approaches for liquidity
- Consider advanced charitable planning techniques
- Implement trust strategies for income and estate tax planning
- Develop comprehensive business exit tax planning
- Maximize available business deductions and credits
- Implement multi-entity strategies when appropriate

Pre-Retirement Phase Tax Strategy

In the years approaching retirement, focus on positioning assets for tax-efficient distribution and transfer.

Key strategies:

- Develop comprehensive Roth conversion strategy
- Implement strategic tax loss harvesting
- Consider partial business exit strategies with optimal tax treatment
- Establish basis management plan for appreciated assets
- Finalize estate and wealth transfer framework
- Implement asset location optimization across accounts
- Develop tax-efficient charitable giving plan

Distribution Phase Tax Strategy

During retirement, focus on withdrawal strategies that minimize taxation while maximizing legacy potential.

Key strategies:

- Implement tax-bracket management for withdrawals
- Coordinate Social Security claiming with tax planning
- Develop required minimum distribution strategies
- Implement qualified charitable distribution approaches
- Finalize basis step-up planning for inherited assets
- Consider life insurance for tax-efficient wealth transfer
- Evaluate partial Roth conversions in lower-income years

For the Johnson family we advised, implementing phase-appropriate tax strategies created substantial benefits throughout their financial journey. During their peak earning years, they focused on maximizing business structures and retirement contributions. In pre-retirement, they implemented a systematic Roth conversion strategy over five years. In retirement, they developed a withdrawal sequence that minimized taxation while maximizing legacy potential.

"Having phase-appropriate tax strategies meant we were always optimizing for our current situation rather than using a one-size-fits-all approach," Mr. Johnson explained. "The tax savings compounded over time, dramatically increasing our retirement resources and potential legacy."

Implementing Your Tax Strategy System

Even the best tax strategies fail without proper implementation systems. These systems ensure consistency, compliance, and optimization throughout the year rather than just during tax filing season.

1. The Tax Strategy Team

Effective tax planning typically requires a coordinated team of professionals.

Implementation approach:

- Identify a tax strategist (not just a preparer) as your lead advisor
- Consider specialists for specific areas (real estate, business, trusts, etc.)
- Establish coordination between tax advisors and other financial professionals
- Implement clear communication protocols among team members

- Schedule regular strategy meetings beyond tax preparation season

2. The Tax Planning Calendar

Strategic tax planning requires year-round attention with specific activities at different times.

Implementation elements:

- January-April: Prior year optimization and filing
- May-June: Mid-year strategy review and adjustment
- July-September: Preliminary next-year planning
- October-December: Year-end optimization and implementation
- Monthly: Ongoing monitoring and adjustment as needed

3. Tax Projection Systems

Proactive planning requires forward-looking projections rather than retrospective analysis.

Implementation elements:

- Quarterly tax projections based on current-year activity
- Multi-year projections for strategic planning
- Scenario analysis for major financial decisions
- Regular updates as circumstances change
- Coordination with overall financial projections

4. Documentation and Compliance Systems

Strategic tax planning requires meticulous documentation to withstand potential scrutiny.

Implementation elements:

- Contemporaneous record-keeping for critical activities
- Documentation of business purpose for entity structures
- Support for positions taken on valuations and transactions
- Maintenance of required corporate and entity formalities
- Coordination of international reporting when applicable

5. Tax Strategy Evaluation Metrics

Measuring success goes beyond simply reducing this year's tax bill.

Implementation elements:

- Track effective tax rate over time
- Measure tax savings relative to default scenario
- Calculate tax efficiency of investment returns
- Evaluate present value of deferred tax benefits
- Assess tax strategy costs versus benefits

For Elijah, implementing these systems transformed his approach to taxation. He established:

- A quarterly meeting schedule with his tax strategist
- A documentation system for business activities and deductions
- A tax projection model updated throughout the year

- A coordination protocol between his tax advisor and financial planner
- A tax strategy evaluation dashboard tracking his progress

"Having systems in place meant my tax strategy became a continuous process rather than an annual event," Elijah noted. "I'm making tax-optimized decisions throughout the year rather than just discovering the consequences at tax time."

The Family Tax Strategy

For families building generational wealth, a coordinated family tax approach creates substantial advantages beyond individual planning.

Multi-Generational Tax Planning

Strategic tax implementation across generations can create significant financial leverage.

Family Entity Structures

Implementation approach:

- Establish family limited partnerships or LLCs for investments
- Implement family management companies where appropriate
- Consider family private trust companies in appropriate situations
- Develop family charitable structures (foundations, donor-advised funds)
- Implement family banking strategies with tax advantages

Coordinated Individual Planning

Implementation approach:

Implementation approach:

- Coordinate individual tax situations across family members
- Implement strategic gifting between generations
- Develop family business succession with tax efficiency
- Consider generation-skipping strategies for appropriate assets
- Structure education funding with optimal tax treatment

Family Tax Education

Implementation approach:

- Develop age-appropriate tax education for all family members
- Create documentation explaining the strategic purpose of family tax structures
- Include tax understanding in broader financial literacy development
- Ensure multiple family members understand tax strategy implications
- Establish continuity planning for tax strategies

CHAPTER 8: CREATE A TAX WEALTH STRATEGY

For the Rodriguez family we advised, their multi-generational tax strategy transformed how they approached both wealth building and preservation. They established:

- A family limited partnership for investment assets with strategic distributions
- A systematic gifting program utilizing lifetime exemptions
- A family education system teaching tax principles to the next generation
- Coordinated business entity structures maximizing family tax advantages
- A family foundation for tax-efficient charitable impact

"We've created a tax strategy ecosystem rather than just individual plans," Mrs. Rodriguez explained. "Each family member's tax situation is considered as part of the whole, with structures that benefit the entire family across generations."

Elijah: Three Years Later

Let's revisit Elijah's journey three years after implementing his comprehensive tax strategy.

His transformation has been remarkable:

Strategic Implementation:

- Fully optimized his S-Corporation structure for his consulting business
- Implemented a defined benefit plan alongside his 401(k)

- Established a systematic real estate investment approach with tax advantages
- Created a family limited partnership for investment assets
- Implemented strategic income timing between tax years

Financial Impact:

- Reduced his effective tax rate from 38% to 22%
- Increased his annual investment capacity by over $40,000
- Built a real estate portfolio creating both cash flow and tax advantages
- Established tax-advantaged college funding for his children
- Created a coordinated estate plan with minimal transfer tax exposure

Knowledge Evolution:

- From viewing taxes as an inevitable expense, he developed sophisticated understanding of tax planning as a wealth-building tool
- He began educating colleagues about strategic tax approaches
- He implemented quarterly tax planning meetings coordinated with his overall financial strategy
- He developed specific multi-year tax projections guiding major financial decisions

"The shift in perspective changed everything," Elijah reflected. "I used to focus on earning more, then be frustrated by how much went to taxes. Now I focus on keeping more of what I earn through strategic planning. The impact on our wealth trajectory has been transformative."

Most importantly, Elijah's relationship with taxation fundamentally changed. Rather than viewing taxes as an inevitable expense to be minimized only at filing time, he now understands tax planning as a year-round strategic process integrated with his overall wealth-building plan.

Your Tax Strategy Journey

As we conclude this chapter, remember that strategic tax planning represents one of the most significant opportunities to accelerate your wealth-building journey. Every dollar saved through legitimate tax strategy is a dollar that can be directed toward building assets rather than funding government operations.

Whether you're just beginning to explore tax strategy like Elijah initially was, or looking to optimize an existing approach, the principles in this chapter provide a framework for keeping more of what you earn. Start where you are, implement one strategy at a time, and coordinate your tax approach with your overall wealth-building plan.

For Black families building generational wealth, strategic tax planning creates particularly significant advantages. Given historical barriers to wealth accumulation, we cannot afford to lose unnecessary dollars to taxation. Implementing sophisticated, legitimate tax strategies helps level the playing field while creating new possibilities for current and future generations.

In the next chapter, we'll explore how to establish your legacy through comprehensive estate planning, ensuring that the wealth you've built benefits future generations with minimal erosion from taxes, fees, or family conflict. But first, complete the action steps below to begin optimizing your tax approach.

ACTION STEP: Schedule a Consultation with a Tax Professional

- **Evaluate your current tax position**
  - Calculate your effective tax rate for the past three years
  - Identify your primary sources of taxation (income, self-employment, capital gains, etc.)
  - Document deductions and credits you're currently utilizing
  - Determine your marginal tax bracket and impact of additional income
  - Identify areas where you suspect tax inefficiency
- **Select a tax strategy professional**
  - Interview tax professionals focused on planning, not just compliance
  - Confirm experience with situations similar to yours
  - Verify knowledge in specific areas relevant to your situation
  - Discuss fee structure for strategic planning versus preparation
  - Establish expectations for ongoing planning versus annual filing
- **Prepare for your strategy consultation**
  - Compile the last two years of tax returns for review
  - Document major anticipated financial changes (income, business, investments)

CHAPTER 8: CREATE A TAX WEALTH STRATEGY

- [ ] Prepare specific questions about potential strategies
- [ ] Consider your lifestyle flexibility for implementing various strategies
- [ ] Define your tax strategy objectives beyond simply reducing current taxes
- [ ] **Develop your strategic tax plan**
  - [ ] Identify immediate optimization opportunities
  - [ ] Create medium-term strategic shifts in structures or approaches
  - [ ] Develop long-term planning for wealth transfer and estate considerations
  - [ ] Establish implementation timeline with specific action items
  - [ ] Define coordination requirements with other advisors
- [ ] **Implement your tax management system**
  - [ ] Schedule regular tax planning meetings (at least quarterly)
  - [ ] Create documentation protocols for tax-relevant activities
  - [ ] Establish monitoring systems for changing tax legislation
  - [ ] Implement tax projection tools for ongoing management
  - [ ] Coordinate tax planning with overall financial calendar

Remember: Strategic tax planning is a continuous process, not an annual event. The most effective approaches integrate tax considerations into daily financial decisions throughout the year, creating significant advantages that compound over time.

CHAPTER 9

ESTABLISH LEGACY

"Someone is sitting in the shade today because someone planted a tree a long time ago."
—Warren Buffett

"I've worked so hard to build what we have. The thought of it being wasted, squandered, or causing family conflict after I'm gone keeps me up at night."

These words came from Eleanor, a successful entrepreneur in her early sixties who had built a seven-figure business from scratch while raising three children as a single mother. Through discipline, sacrifice, and strategic decision-making, she had accumulated significant assets—her business, investment portfolio, and several real estate properties.

But as retirement approached, Eleanor realized she had focused almost exclusively on building wealth without adequate attention to protecting and transferring it. Her estate planning consisted only of a simple will drafted years earlier, with no protections against taxes, probate costs, or potential family disagreements.

"I want my children and grandchildren to benefit from what I've built," she explained, "but I don't want it to be diminished by unnecessary taxes or legal fees. And more importantly, I want it to be a blessing rather than a source of conflict or entitlement."

Eleanor's concerns highlight a crucial reality that many successful wealth builders discover: creating wealth is only part of the journey. Ensuring that wealth becomes a lasting legacy that empowers rather than hinders future generations requires intentional planning and structure. This final critical step is why "Establish Legacy" is the ninth component of our Abundance Formula.

Beyond Estate Planning: The Legacy Mindset

Traditional estate planning focuses primarily on the technical aspects of wealth transfer—minimizing taxes and fees while ensuring assets pass to intended beneficiaries. While these technical elements are essential, truly effective legacy planning encompasses a much broader vision.

The Estate Plan vs. Legacy Plan Paradigm

The difference between these approaches is profound:

Estate Plan (Technical):

- Focuses on asset distribution mechanics
- Emphasizes tax and probate avoidance
- Addresses primarily financial assets
- Operates through legal documents

- Primarily addresses what happens after death
- Limited to financial and legal considerations

Legacy Plan (Comprehensive):

- Focuses on values, purpose, and impact
- Emphasizes family harmony and empowerment
- Addresses financial, intellectual, social, and spiritual capital
- Operates through both documents and ongoing family processes
- Actively functions during life and after death
- Integrates financial, relational, and philosophical dimensions

This shift from technical estate planning to comprehensive legacy planning represents the difference between simply transferring assets and truly establishing a multi-generational legacy that strengthens and empowers your family.

The Four Dimensions of Legacy Capital

A truly comprehensive legacy plan addresses four distinct types of capital:

1. **Financial Capital:** Monetary assets, properties, businesses, investments, and other economic resources
2. **Intellectual Capital:** Knowledge, skills, expertise, education, and wisdom accumulated through experience
3. **Social Capital:** Relationships, networks, connections, reputation, and community standing
4. **Spiritual/Values Capital:** Core principles, ethical frameworks, faith traditions, and fundamental beliefs

Most traditional planning addresses only financial capital, leaving the other three dimensions—which often prove more valuable and lasting—to chance or informal transmission. Comprehensive legacy planning intentionally addresses all four dimensions, creating systems for their preservation and transfer.

Creating Your Family's Wealth Mission Statement

The foundation of effective legacy planning is clarity about purpose—why are you building wealth, and what do you want it to accomplish beyond your lifetime? A carefully crafted family wealth mission statement provides this essential foundation.

The Purpose of a Family Wealth Mission Statement

This document serves several crucial functions:

1. **Provides direction** for financial decisions and wealth structures
2. **Creates alignment** among family members around shared purpose
3. **Establishes criteria** for evaluating opportunities and priorities
4. **Guides trustees and advisors** when making decisions on the family's behalf
5. **Anchors future generations** in the founding vision
6. **Defines success** beyond simply preserving or growing assets

Without this foundational clarity, even the most technically perfect estate plan may fail to achieve your deeper intentions for your wealth and family.

Key Components of an Effective Mission Statement

While each family's statement should be unique, effective wealth mission statements typically address:

1. Core Values

Identify the fundamental principles that guide your family's approach to wealth, such as:

- Stewardship vs. ownership perspective
- Education and continuous learning
- Work ethic and contribution
- Philanthropy and community responsibility
- Faith or spiritual foundations
- Family unity and support

2. Wealth Purpose

Articulate why your family has wealth and what it should accomplish:

- Creating opportunity vs. creating comfort
- Supporting individual growth and potential
- Fostering independence vs. enabling dependence
- Serving needs beyond the family

- Preserving cultural or family heritage
- Creating meaningful work or contribution

3. Legacy Vision

Describe the long-term impact you hope your wealth will have:

- Impact on individual family members
- Influence within your community
- Continuation of business or philanthropic efforts
- Preservation of specific values or traditions
- Timeline perspective (generations vs. years)
- Balance between preservation and utilization

4. Governance Principles

Outline how wealth-related decisions should be made:

- Roles and participation of various family members
- Balance between unity and individual autonomy
- Transparency vs. privacy considerations
- Conflict resolution approaches
- Adaptation and evolution over time
- Integration of non-family advisors or trustees

CHAPTER 9: ESTABLISH LEGACY

The Mission Statement Development Process

Creating an effective family wealth mission statement involves several key steps:

1. **Personal reflection:** Begin with individual reflection on values, hopes, and concerns related to wealth
2. **Family dialogue:** Engage in structured conversations with family members about their perspectives
3. **Draft development:** Create initial drafts incorporating input from all stakeholders
4. **External perspective:** Consider input from trusted advisors who understand your family dynamics
5. **Refinement process:** Revise through multiple iterations until it resonates with all family members
6. **Formal adoption:** Ceremonially affirm the statement as a family
7. **Regular review:** Revisit periodically (every 3-5 years) to ensure continued relevance

For Eleanor, developing a family wealth mission statement transformed her approach to legacy planning. Through facilitated family discussions, she and her children articulated a mission centered on education, entrepreneurship, and community impact. This statement became the foundation for all subsequent legal and financial structures.

"The process itself was as valuable as the document we created," Eleanor reflected. "For the first time, we had deeply meaningful conversations about what our wealth meant to us as a family and what we wanted it to accomplish beyond financial security."

Trusts, Wills, and Estate Planning Essentials

With your family wealth mission as foundation, the technical aspects of estate planning provide the structure to implement your vision effectively.

Wills vs. Trusts: Strategic Considerations

Understanding the distinct roles of these fundamental planning tools is essential:

Last Will and Testament

Key functions:

- Names executors to manage estate settlement
- Designates guardians for minor children
- Provides instructions for asset distribution
- Expresses final wishes regarding arrangements
- Creates testamentary trusts that arise after death
- Addresses personal property distribution

Limitations:

- Requires probate process (public, potentially costly and time-consuming)
- Becomes effective only at death, providing no incapacity protection
- May trigger state inheritance taxes in certain jurisdictions
- Offers limited control over how assets are used after distribution

- Provides minimal protection from beneficiaries' creditors or divorces
- Creates potential for will contests in contentious situations

Revocable Living Trusts

Key functions:

- Avoids probate process for properly funded assets
- Provides management continuity during incapacity
- Maintains privacy regarding asset distribution
- Creates framework for ongoing asset management
- Often contains tax planning provisions
- Reduces potential grounds for family disputes

Limitations:

- Requires proper funding during lifetime to be effective
- Provides no asset protection for the creator (grantor)
- Offers no tax advantages during grantor's lifetime
- Creates administrative requirements for maintenance
- May still leave assets vulnerable to beneficiaries' issues without proper provisions
- Typically more expensive to establish than simple wills

Strategic Implementation Considerations

Most comprehensive estate plans incorporate both wills and trusts, with specific strategies based on:

1. **Asset complexity and value:** More complex or valuable estates typically benefit more from trust-centered planning
2. **Privacy concerns:** Individuals with stronger privacy preferences generally favor trust-centered approaches
3. **Family dynamics:** Complicated family situations (blended families, special needs, addiction issues) typically require more sophisticated trust structures
4. **State of residence:** Estate laws and probate processes vary significantly by state, affecting the relative advantages of different approaches
5. **Business interests:** Ownership in private businesses often necessitates more sophisticated planning structures
6. **Control preferences:** Individuals desiring greater posthumous control typically benefit from trust-centered planning

For most families building significant wealth, a revocable living trust serves as the centerpiece of the estate plan, with a "pour-over will" as backup for any assets not properly transferred to the trust during lifetime.

Specialized Trust Strategies

Beyond basic revocable living trusts, several specialized trust structures serve specific purposes in comprehensive legacy planning:

1. Irrevocable Life Insurance Trusts (ILITs)

These trusts own life insurance policies, keeping proceeds outside the taxable estate while providing liquidity for taxes or other needs.

Implementation strategy:

- Establish trust before applying for new policies
- Transfer existing policies carefully, mindful of three-year lookback rules
- Structure premium funding through annual exclusion gifts when possible
- Select trustees with appropriate insurance knowledge
- Coordinate with overall estate liquidity needs

2. Dynasty Trusts

These long-term trusts extend wealth protection for multiple generations, potentially in perpetuity in certain jurisdictions.

Implementation strategy:

- Establish in jurisdictions with favorable rule against perpetuity provisions
- Allocate generation-skipping transfer tax exemptions efficiently

- Structure for maximum flexibility given long time horizons
- Create appropriate governance mechanisms for future decision-making
- Balance control with adaptability for changing circumstances

3. Charitable Remainder Trusts (CRTs)

These split-interest trusts provide income to non-charitable beneficiaries for a period, with remaining assets going to charity, creating current tax deductions and philanthropic impact.

Implementation strategy:

- Fund with appreciated assets to maximize tax benefits
- Select appropriate payout structure and rate based on objectives
- Balance income needs against desired ultimate charitable impact
- Consider companion wealth replacement strategies with life insurance
- Coordinate with overall philanthropic and tax planning

4. Qualified Personal Residence Trusts (QPRTs)

These specialized trusts allow transfer of a residence at a discounted gift tax value while retaining the right to live in the home for a specified term.

Implementation strategy:

- Select appropriate term based on life expectancy and objectives
- Consider fractional interest transfers for larger properties
- Plan for post-term occupancy arrangements if desired

5. Special Needs Trusts

These trusts provide for beneficiaries with disabilities without disqualifying them from essential government benefits.

Implementation strategy:

- Structure as either first-party or third-party based on funding source
- Include provisions that complement rather than replace government benefits
- Select trustees with understanding of benefit programs and special needs
- Provide detailed guidance on quality-of-life intentions
- Coordinate with other family members' planning for consistency

6. Incentive Trusts

These structures include provisions that encourage certain behaviors or achievements while discouraging others.

Implementation strategy:

- Align incentives with family mission and values
- Balance specificity with flexibility for changing circumstances

- Consider objective and measurable standards when possible
- Include trustee discretion to address unanticipated situations
- Build in regular review and potential modification procedures

Strategic Beneficiary Designations

Beyond wills and trusts, beneficiary designations on financial accounts and insurance policies form a crucial component of effective estate planning.

Implementation considerations:

- Review all beneficiary designations regularly (at least annually)
- Ensure coordination between designations and overall estate plan
- Consider tax implications, particularly for retirement accounts
- Understand the limitations of certain beneficiary options
- Use contingent beneficiaries appropriately
- Evaluate per stirpes vs. per capita designations based on family situation

Incapacity Planning

Comprehensive legacy planning addresses potential incapacity, not just eventual death.

Essential components:

- Durable power of attorney for financial matters
- Healthcare power of attorney
- HIPAA authorization forms

- Living will/advance directives
- Standby guardianship designations for minor children
- Business continuity provisions if applicable

For Eleanor, implementing these technical components created a comprehensive structure aligned with her family wealth mission. She established a revocable living trust as her primary planning tool, with specialized provisions for her business interests and real estate holdings. She also created an irrevocable life insurance trust to provide liquidity for estate taxes while keeping the proceeds outside her taxable estate.

"Having these structures in place gave me tremendous peace of mind," Eleanor shared. "Not just because they addressed technical concerns like taxes and probate, but because they created a framework for implementing our family's deeper intentions for our wealth."

Teaching Financial Literacy to the Next Generation

Perhaps the most commonly overlooked aspect of legacy planning is preparing heirs to receive and manage wealth responsibly. Without this preparation, even the most technically perfect wealth transfer plan may ultimately fail.

The Three-Phase Approach to Heir Preparation

Effective preparation typically involves three progressive phases:

Phase 1: Financial Literacy Foundation (Ages 5-12)

During childhood, focus on building basic understanding of money concepts.

Implementation strategies:

- Implement age-appropriate allowance systems tied to responsibilities
- Open savings accounts and teach basic banking concepts
- Use transparent family discussions about spending decisions and tradeoffs
- Introduce basic concepts of earning, saving, spending, and giving
- Create experiential learning through supervised money management
- Use games, books, and activities that teach financial concepts

Phase 2: Financial Responsibility Development (Ages 13-22)

During adolescence and early adulthood, focus on building practical skills and personal responsibility.

Implementation strategies:

- Provide increasing responsibility for personal financial decisions
- Teach budgeting and planning skills with real consequences

- Introduce investment concepts through actual (though modest) investing
- Include in discussions about family financial decisions as appropriate
- Create earning opportunities connected to family business or investments
- Support education regarding taxes, credit, insurance, and other practical matters
- Implement matching programs for entrepreneurial or philanthropic initiatives

Phase 3: Wealth Stewardship Preparation (Ages 23+)

As young adults mature, focus on preparing them for their role in family wealth stewardship.

Implementation strategies:

- Gradually reveal details about family wealth as responsibility is demonstrated
- Provide guided exposure to family professional advisors
- Include in family governance meetings with defined roles
- Support advanced financial education through courses or mentorship
- Create opportunities for meaningful input on family philanthropic decisions
- Develop individual connection to family wealth mission
- Implement apprenticeship in family business or investment activities

Addressing the "Sudden Wealth Syndrome"

Heirs unprepared for significant inheritance often experience what psychologists call "sudden wealth syndrome"—a set of challenges including identity confusion, relationship complications, and decision paralysis.

Prevention strategies:

- Create graduated access to inherited assets rather than lump-sum distributions
- Provide pre-inheritance experiences with meaningful amounts of money
- Ensure heirs have developed identity and purpose independent of family wealth
- Establish mentoring relationships with trustworthy advisors
- Prepare heirs for the emotional and psychological aspects of inheritance
- Develop peer connections with others in similar situations
- Implement post-inheritance support systems

Building Financial Capability Through Experience

Beyond formal education, practical experience proves essential for developing true financial capability.

Implementation approaches:

- Create "apprenticeship" opportunities in family business or investing activities

- Establish dedicated investment pools for next-generation management
- Implement family bank programs for entrepreneurial initiatives
- Develop philanthropic funds directed by next-generation family members
- Create structured opportunities to observe parents/grandparents making financial decisions
- Support formal business or investment education
- Provide coaching through initial financial mistakes in safe environments

For Eleanor, implementing a structured financial literacy program transformed her confidence about her children's readiness to manage their inheritance. She established regular family financial discussions, created a family investment committee including her adult children, and developed a "family bank" to support entrepreneurial initiatives.

"Teaching them wasn't just about the mechanics of money management," Eleanor noted. "It was about helping them develop a healthy relationship with wealth—seeing it as a tool for creating opportunity and impact rather than simply providing comfort or status. That perspective shift has been more valuable than any specific financial knowledge."

Lessons from the Rockefeller Family's Approach to Legacy Building

The Rockefeller family stands as one of history's most successful examples of wealth preservation across multiple generations. Their approach provides valuable insights for families at any wealth level seeking to establish lasting legacies.

Key Principles from the Rockefeller Legacy System

Several fundamental principles distinguish the Rockefeller approach:

1. Values-Centered Wealth Philosophy

The Rockefeller family established clear values that guided wealth decisions across generations.

Implementation elements:

- Formal articulation of family values and purpose
- Regular family meetings reinforcing these values
- Storytelling that connects family history to core principles
- Consistent demonstration of values through action
- Integration of values into all wealth structures and decisions

2. Family Governance Structures

Rather than leaving family decision-making to chance, the Rockefellers created formal governance systems.

Implementation elements:

- Regular family assemblies with all members
- Family council for executive decision-making
- Specialized committees for different wealth aspects

- Clear roles, responsibilities, and authorities
- Documented policies and procedures
- Conflict resolution mechanisms
- Integration of non-family expertise when needed

3. Individual Development Focus

The family emphasized developing each member's potential rather than simply preserving wealth.

Implementation elements:

- Support for education aligned with individual interests and talents
- Encouragement of entrepreneurial initiatives
- Expectation of meaningful work and contribution
- Balanced perspective on wealth as enabler rather than end goal
- Personal mentoring and development resources
- Celebration of individual achievements beyond wealth

4. Philanthropic Engagement

Philanthropy served as both wealth purpose and family unification mechanism.

Implementation elements:

- Structured family giving vehicles
- Next-generation involvement in philanthropic decisions
- Balance between collective and individual giving interests

- Integration of service beyond financial contributions
- Use of philanthropy for family member development
- Connection of giving to family values and history

5. Professional Management with Family Oversight

The family balanced professional expertise with family direction.

Implementation elements:

- Family office structure for wealth management
- Clear separation between family and management roles
- Defined communication and reporting systems
- Performance metrics aligned with family values
- Integration of family members in oversight roles
- Ongoing education for family members to enable effective oversight

6. Intentional Communication Systems

Rather than avoiding discussions about wealth, the family created intentional communication frameworks.

Implementation elements:

- Regular structured family meetings
- Defined information sharing protocols
- Education about wealth structures and purposes
- Safe spaces for questions and concerns
- Conflict management processes

- Celebration of family history and traditions
- Cross-generational relationship building

Adapting Rockefeller Principles at Different Wealth Levels

While the Rockefeller fortune enabled elaborate structures, their core principles can be adapted at any wealth level:

For emerging wealth families:

- Begin with clear articulation of wealth purpose and values
- Implement regular family discussions about financial decisions
- Create simple but intentional governance for family assets
- Establish family philanthropy, even at modest levels
- Develop next-generation financial education early
- Document intentions and lessons learned

For established wealth families:

- Formalize family governance structures
- Consider family office services (either dedicated or multi-family)
- Implement more sophisticated education for family members
- Develop formal communication systems and regular meetings
- Create structured next-generation involvement opportunities
- Consider professional facilitation for important family processes

For Eleanor, adapting Rockefeller principles to her family's situation meant implementing quarterly family meetings, establishing a family council including her adult children, creating a family philanthropy fund with shared decision-making, and documenting her wealth philosophy and intentions.

"We don't have Rockefeller-level wealth," Eleanor acknowledged, "but we can certainly apply their principles of intentionality, governance, and values-centered decision making. These approaches work at any wealth level—it's about the mindset, not the millions."

Integrating Life Insurance into Your Estate Plan

As discussed in the previous chapter, properly structured life insurance serves as a powerful tool in comprehensive legacy planning, addressing several critical needs:

Estate Liquidity Provision

For estates potentially subject to estate taxes, life insurance provides essential liquidity to pay these taxes without forcing the liquidation of other assets like businesses or real estate.

Implementation strategy:

- Calculate potential estate tax liability based on current net worth and growth projections

- Structure life insurance outside the taxable estate through proper trust ownership
- Ensure the policy face amount covers projected estate tax liability plus administrative costs
- Review and adjust coverage as net worth changes over time
- Coordinate premium funding with gift tax planning

Wealth Replacement Strategies

Life insurance can effectively "replace" assets directed elsewhere, such as charitable gifts or assets allocated to specific heirs.

Implementation examples:

- Replace value of business interest going to involved children for non-involved children
- Replace value of real estate properties allocated based on geographic proximity
- Replace assets donated to charity through charitable remainder trusts
- Replace assets sold to intentionally defective grantor trusts
- Replace value of qualified plan assets diminished by income taxation

Estate Equalization

When certain assets (particularly businesses or real estate) will pass to specific heirs, life insurance can provide equivalent value to other heirs.

Implementation strategy:

- Calculate appropriate insurance face amount based on asset valuations
- Structure ownership to avoid inclusion in the taxable estate
- Consider survivorship policies for married couples to reduce premium costs
- Coordinate with overall estate division intentions
- Review coverage as asset values change over time

Legacy Enhancement

Beyond solving specific technical issues, life insurance can simply increase the total legacy transferred to heirs or charitable interests.

Implementation strategy:

- Structure policies for maximum long-term efficiency
- Consider permanent coverage with guaranteed provisions
- Evaluate leverage created through premium-to-death-benefit ratio
- Coordinate beneficiary designations with overall estate plan
- Implement trust ownership when control or protection is desired

CHAPTER 9: ESTABLISH LEGACY

Strategic Implementation Considerations

Several key factors determine optimal life insurance integration in estate planning:

1. **Ownership structure:** Individual, trust, corporate, or partnership ownership creates significantly different outcomes for tax, control, and access purposes.
2. **Product design:** Different policy types (term, whole life, universal life, variable, indexed) serve different estate planning objectives with varying efficiency.
3. **Premium funding:** Various approaches to premium payment (annual gifts, financing, existing asset repositioning) create different planning implications.
4. **Beneficiary design:** Direct beneficiary designations versus trust-based death benefits create different control, protection, and distribution options.
5. **Policy management:** Ongoing evaluation and potential optimization of insurance policies ensures continued alignment with evolving estate planning objectives.

For Eleanor, life insurance served multiple functions in her legacy plan. She established an irrevocable life insurance trust owning a $3 million policy, providing liquidity for estate taxes while creating an immediate pool of assets for her grandchildren's education. She also used a survivorship policy to equalize inheritances between the child active in her business and her other children.

"The life insurance created solutions to several planning challenges simultaneously," Eleanor explained. "It provided immediate liquidity, equalized inheritances, and created specific pools of money for different purposes—all while leveraging relatively modest premium payments into significant benefits."

The Family Legacy Protection System

Beyond legal structures and financial tools, a comprehensive legacy plan requires ongoing systems to maintain and strengthen family cohesion across generations.

Family Meeting Structures

Regular, purposeful family gatherings form the cornerstone of sustained legacy success.

Implementation elements:

- Annual or semi-annual full family assemblies
- Quarterly family council meetings for representative decision-making
- Structured agendas balancing business and relationship components
- Defined roles (facilitator, secretary, timekeeper, etc.)
- Intentional inclusion of all generations as appropriate
- Documentation of decisions and action items
- Balance between formal and informal interaction
- Progressive involvement of younger generations

Family Education Systems

Ongoing education tailored to family members' developmental stages sustains knowledge and capability.

Implementation elements:

- Age-appropriate financial education curriculum
- Family history and values transmission
- Structured exposure to family advisors and resources
- Mentoring relationships across generations
- External educational resources and experiences
- Documentation of family knowledge and wisdom
- Regular assessment of educational needs

Family Communication Protocols

Clear communication expectations prevent misunderstandings that threaten family cohesion.

Implementation elements:

- Defined information sharing standards and limitations
- Regular written updates on family financial matters
- Clear processes for raising questions or concerns
- Established conflict resolution pathways
- Transparency appropriate to family members' roles and responsibilities
- Balance between privacy and openness
- Technology platforms for secure information sharing

Family Governance Documentation

Written governance documents provide clarity and continuity for family decision-making.

Implementation elements:

- Family constitution or charter outlining overall governance
- Specific policies for different aspects of family wealth
- Decision-making authorities and processes
- Membership criteria for various family entities
- Amendment processes for adapting to changing circumstances
- Conflict resolution procedures
- Relationship to legal entities and documents

Family Heritage Preservation

Intentional preservation of family history and traditions strengthens identity and purpose across generations.

Implementation elements:

- Documentation of family stories and history
- Preservation of significant artifacts and memorabilia
- Regular celebration of family traditions
- Creation of shared experiences that become new traditions
- Integration of family history into governance and education
- Digital archives of family documents and photographs
- Intentional transmission of family wisdom and values

For Eleanor, implementing these systems transformed her confidence about her legacy's longevity. She established quarterly family meetings with structured agendas, created a family knowledge base documenting everything from investment philosophy to cherished recipes, implemented a family council with representation from each family branch, and developed a family education program addressing both financial and values-based topics.

"The systems make our intentions sustainable," Eleanor reflected. "Without them, even the best legal documents and financial structures would eventually lose their connection to our family's purpose. The systems keep our legacy alive in our daily relationships and decisions."

Eleanor: Three Years Later

Let's revisit Eleanor's journey three years after implementing her comprehensive legacy plan.

Her transformation has been remarkable:

Technical Implementation:

- Established a revocable living trust with specialized provisions for her business
- Created an irrevocable life insurance trust for estate liquidity
- Implemented a family limited partnership for investment assets
- Developed a business succession plan with appropriate legal structures
- Coordinated all beneficiary designations with her overall plan

Family Preparation:

- Instituted quarterly family meetings with educational components
- Created a family council with defined decision-making authority
- Established a family philanthropy committee with next-generation leadership
- Implemented a financial literacy curriculum for grandchildren
- Developed a family knowledge base documenting values, history, and wisdom

Legacy Protection:

- Created a detailed letter of wishes providing context for legal documents
- Recorded video messages sharing values and intentions for various assets
- Established relationships between her children and key advisors
- Funded educational trusts for grandchildren with defined purpose
- Implemented a family governance document outlining decision processes

Personal Transformation:

- From anxiety about wealth transfer to confidence in legacy sustainability
- From focus solely on technical planning to emphasis on family preparation

CHAPTER 9: ESTABLISH LEGACY

- From informal family financial discussions to structured governance systems
- From concern about potential family conflict to trust in established processes

"Three years ago, I had built significant wealth but had no real confidence it would become a lasting positive legacy," Eleanor reflected. "Now I have not only the technical structures to transfer wealth efficiently, but the family systems to ensure it fulfills its purpose across generations. The peace of mind that brings is perhaps my greatest achievement."

Your Legacy Establishment Journey

As we conclude this final chapter of The Abundance Formula, remember that establishing your legacy represents the culmination of all previous wealth-building steps. Without careful attention to how your wealth will transition and what impact it will have beyond your lifetime, even the most successful wealth accumulation can fail to achieve its deeper purpose.

Whether you're just beginning to consider legacy planning or looking to enhance existing structures, the principles in this chapter provide a framework for ensuring your wealth creates the impact you intend. Start where you are, implement one element at a time, and remember that legacy planning is an ongoing process rather than a one-time event.

For Black families building generational wealth, intentional legacy planning takes on particular significance. Given historical barriers to wealth creation and transfer, we cannot afford to leave the transition of hard-won assets to chance or incomplete planning. By implementing comprehensive legacy structures and systems, we create the foundation for multigenerational prosperity that can help close the persistent racial wealth gap while empowering future generations with both resources and wisdom.

As you implement your own legacy plan, remember Eleanor's journey—from successful wealth accumulation but legacy uncertainty to comprehensive systems ensuring both technical efficiency and family preparation. With intentional planning, your wealth can become not just a transferred asset but a true legacy that empowers and strengthens your family for generations to come.

ACTION STEP: Draft or Update Your Will and Explore Setting Up a Trust

- **Assess your current legacy planning status**
    - Inventory existing estate planning documents and when they were last updated
    - Identify gaps in your current planning based on this chapter
    - Evaluate whether your planning aligns with your wealth mission and values
    - Review beneficiary designations on all financial accounts and insurance policies
    - Evaluate your family's preparedness for eventual wealth transfer
    - Identify potential tax or probate issues in your current plan

CHAPTER 9: ESTABLISH LEGACY

- [ ] **Define your legacy planning objectives**
    - [ ] Articulate your wealth transfer goals and priorities
    - [ ] Identify specific concerns about heirs, assets, or potential challenges
    - [ ] Clarify your philosophy regarding inheritance timing and structure
    - [ ] Determine your protection priorities (taxes, creditors, family conflict, etc.)
    - [ ] Consider charitable or community impact intentions
- [ ] **Select appropriate professional guidance**
    - [ ] Identify estate planning attorneys with experience relevant to your situation
    - [ ] Consider whether specialized advisors are needed (business succession, etc.)
    - [ ] Evaluate the need for financial advisors with estate planning expertise
    - [ ] Consider family dynamics facilitators if complex relationships exist
    - [ ] Establish expectations for ongoing planning versus one-time document creation
- [ ] **Develop your core estate planning documents**
    - [ ] Create or update your will with current intentions
    - [ ] Evaluate whether trusts are appropriate for your situation
    - [ ] Establish or update powers of attorney for financial and healthcare matters
    - [ ] Create or review advance healthcare directives
    - [ ] Ensure guardian designations for minor children are current

- [ ] Develop supporting documentation explaining your intentions
- [ ] **Implement your family legacy system**
  - [ ] Schedule your first formal family meeting
  - [ ] Begin developing your family wealth mission statement
  - [ ] Create a simple family education plan appropriate to current ages
  - [ ] Establish regular review dates for your estate planning documents
  - [ ] Communicate appropriate elements of your plan to family members
  - [ ] Begin documenting family history, values, and wisdom

Remember: Legacy planning is ultimately about people, not just documents or assets. While technical structures are essential, the most successful legacies combine proper legal planning with intentional family preparation and clear communication of values and purpose. The time invested in this final step of The Abundance Formula ensures that all your previous wealth-building efforts create lasting positive impact beyond your lifetime.

CHAPTER 10

EMPOWERING THE COMMUNITY

"If you want to go quickly, go alone. If you want to go far, go together."
—African Proverb

"I've achieved financial success, but when I look at my community, I don't see my success reflected there. It feels incomplete somehow."

This realization came from Marcus, a technology executive who had built substantial personal wealth through his career and investments. After conscientiously applying wealth-building principles for two decades, he had achieved what many would consider financial freedom—a multi-million-dollar investment portfolio, a beautiful debt-free home, and the ability to retire decades earlier than most.

Yet despite his personal financial achievements, Marcus felt a growing disconnect between his individual success and the economic struggles he witnessed in his broader community.

"I grew up in a neighborhood where few people owned businesses or investment properties," Marcus explained. "After achieving my own financial goals, I realized something important was missing. My individual success means little if my community continues to struggle. True abundance isn't just personal—it's collective."

Marcus's insight highlights a crucial truth that many successful Black wealth-builders discover: while individual financial achievement is essential, lasting prosperity requires extending wealth-building knowledge and opportunity throughout our communities. This broader vision of abundance is why "Empowering the Community" forms the tenth and final component of our Abundance Formula.

Beyond Individual Success: The Group Economics Paradigm

The concept of group economics—cooperative economic activity within a community—has deep roots in African and African-American history. From traditional African village economies to mutual aid societies during Reconstruction to the cooperative movements of the Civil Rights era, collective economic empowerment has been a consistent strategy for community advancement.

The Individual Success vs. Group Economics Paradigm

The difference between these approaches is fundamental:

Individual Success Model:

- Focuses on personal and family wealth accumulation
- Measures achievement through individual financial metrics
- Often requires leaving economically challenged communities
- Creates isolated examples of success
- Relies primarily on individual effort and discipline
- Vulnerable to systemic barriers without collective leverage

Group Economics Model:

- Focuses on community wealth creation and circulation
- Measures success through broader economic indicators
- Strengthens existing communities through investment
- Creates networks of mutual support and opportunity
- Leverages collective resources and capabilities
- Builds power to address systemic barriers effectively

This contrast doesn't suggest abandoning individual wealth-building—indeed, personal financial strength creates the foundation for community contribution. Rather, it proposes that true abundance integrates personal success with community empowerment, creating a mutually reinforcing cycle of prosperity.

The PowerNomics Approach to Group Economics

Dr. Claud Anderson's groundbreaking work in *PowerNomics: The National Plan to Empower Black America* provides a comprehensive framework for implementing group economics principles in modern America. Several key concepts from this work are particularly relevant to wealth-builders seeking to extend their impact:

1. Vertical Integration

Rather than participating in only one segment of the value chain, vertically integrated communities control multiple stages of production, distribution, and sales.

Implementation principles:

- Create businesses that connect to and support each other
- Focus on controlling both supply and distribution channels
- Develop expertise across complementary business sectors
- Reinvest profits into expanding the vertical integration
- Build self-sustaining economic ecosystems within the community

2. Targeted Consumer Support

Strategic consumer spending represents a powerful economic lever when directed intentionally toward community wealth building.

Implementation principles:

- Prioritize businesses owned by community members
- Develop consciousness about spending impacts
- Create visibility and accessibility for community businesses
- Establish standards and accountability for supported businesses
- Balance immediate needs with strategic spending priorities

3. Geographic Concentration

Building economic strength within specific geographic areas creates multiplier effects that accelerate community wealth development.

Implementation principles:

- Focus development efforts within defined neighborhoods
- Create business clusters that draw customers and talent
- Develop commercial real estate to house community businesses
- Invest in enhancing community infrastructure and appeal
- Implement deliberate community wealth circulation strategies

4. Competitive Advantage Identification

Understanding and leveraging unique community strengths creates sustainable economic advantage.

Implementation principles:

- Identify authentic cultural assets with market value
- Develop enterprises aligned with community expertise

- Create barriers to appropriation of community innovations
- Invest in enhancing competitive advantages through education
- Build branding and marketing around authentic strengths

5. Cooperative Investment Structures

Pooling capital creates investment capacity beyond individual resources.

Implementation principles:

- Develop investment clubs and funds with community focus
- Create cooperative ownership structures for larger enterprises
- Implement crowd-funding approaches for community projects
- Establish rotating credit associations for smaller ventures
- Build financial education alongside investment structures

For Marcus, understanding these principles transformed his approach to wealth building. While continuing his personal financial strategy, he began implementing community-focused initiatives: investing in commercial real estate in his childhood neighborhood, creating a business mentorship program for local entrepreneurs, and establishing an investment group focused on community development.

"I realized I needed to expand my definition of financial success," Marcus reflected. "True wealth isn't just having your own needs met—it's creating systems that empower others to build their own prosperity. When I shifted my perspective, I found both greater purpose and, surprisingly, new opportunities that actually accelerated my own financial growth."

CHAPTER 10: EMPOWERING THE COMMUNITY

Supporting and Investing in Black-Owned Businesses

Strategic support for Black-owned businesses creates perhaps the most direct path to community economic empowerment. Beyond simple patronage, comprehensive business support creates multiplier effects that strengthen the entire economic ecosystem.

Strategic Business Support Approaches

Effective business support extends beyond occasional purchases to create sustained impact:

1. Intentional Procurement Practices

For those with influence over business or organizational spending, procurement represents a powerful economic lever.

Implementation strategies:

- Audit current vendor relationships to identify diversification opportunities
- Develop policies establishing minimum targets for Black-owned vendors
- Create mentorship pathways to help promising businesses meet procurement requirements
- Extend payment terms to support smaller businesses' cash flow needs
- Provide feedback and growth opportunities for existing vendors

2. Business-to-Business Networking

Creating connection between Black-owned businesses generates multiple benefits.

Implementation strategies:

- Organize industry-specific networking events focused on business opportunities
- Create formal or informal buying groups to enhance purchasing power
- Develop service exchange programs that leverage complementary capabilities
- Implement referral systems that keep opportunities within the community
- Foster joint venture opportunities for larger projects or contracts

3. Professional Service Access

Many Black-owned businesses struggle to access quality professional services critical for growth.

Implementation strategies:

- Create professional service networks with community commitment
- Develop sliding-scale service models for emerging businesses
- Implement "office hours" programs providing limited free consultation
- Establish service cooperatives sharing costs for needed expertise

- Develop standardized templates and resources for common needs

4. Strategic Angel Investment

Direct investment in promising enterprises provides both capital and expertise.

Implementation strategies:

- Develop investment criteria aligned with community wealth-building
- Create syndication approaches to spread risk while increasing impact
- Implement standardized but flexible investment terms appropriate to early ventures
- Focus on sectors with strong community impact potential
- Balance financial return requirements with community benefit considerations

5. Alternative Funding Models

Beyond traditional investment, innovative funding approaches can address specific community business needs.

Implementation strategies:

- Develop revenue-based financing options tied to business performance

- Create customer pre-purchase programs providing startup capital
- Implement community ownership models spreading both risk and return
- Establish targeted crowdfunding platforms with community focus
- Explore cooperative financing approaches for specific industries

For Kimberly, a healthcare executive we advised, implementing strategic business support transformed both her investment portfolio and community impact. She established a regular procurement review process within her organization, identifying over $2 million in spending that could be redirected to qualified Black-owned businesses. She also joined an angel investment group focused on healthcare technology ventures led by Black entrepreneurs, combining her industry expertise with capital to support promising innovations.

"I realized I had significant influence over capital flows beyond just my personal spending," Kimberly shared. "By being strategic about where both my organization and my investment dollars went, I could help create the ecosystem these businesses needed to thrive. The exciting part is seeing these businesses grow to serve broader markets while maintaining their community connection."

Creating Economic Opportunities Through Mentorship

While capital access represents a critical need, knowledge and relationship capital often prove equally valuable for community economic development. Strategic mentorship creates these intangible but essential assets.

Effective Mentorship Models

Several structured approaches create sustainable mentorship impact:

1. Industry-Specific Mentorship Programs

Focused mentorship within specific sectors creates more actionable guidance and connections.

Implementation strategy:

- Identify industries with both mentorship needs and available mentors
- Create structured programs with clear expectations and commitments
- Develop curriculum addressing sector-specific challenges
- Establish peer support components alongside senior mentorship
- Implement project-based mentorship with tangible outcomes

2. Business Milestone Mentorship

Targeted guidance focused on specific business development phases addresses practical needs.

Implementation strategy:

- Create mentorship teams specialized in startup, growth, and maturity phases
- Develop milestone-specific resource guides and tools
- Implement "just-in-time" mentorship aligned with business evolution
- Establish peer groups of businesses at similar developmental stages
- Provide specialized support for critical transitions (first hire, first location, etc.)

3. Technical Skill Transfer Programs

Focused knowledge transfer in specialized areas builds specific capabilities.

Implementation strategy:

- Identify high-demand technical skills with limited community access
- Develop compressed skill transfer programs with practical application
- Create ongoing support systems for skill implementation
- Establish certification or recognition for program completion
- Build peer teaching components that multiply impact

4. Corporate Partnership Programs

Structured engagement with larger corporations creates both knowledge transfer and market access.

Implementation strategy:

- Identify corporations with both relevant expertise and diversity commitment
- Develop structured programs beyond traditional networking events
- Create specific opportunity pathways within corporate supply chains
- Implement knowledge transfer in both directions (recognizing innovation potential)
- Establish metrics measuring concrete business outcomes

5. Youth Entrepreneurship Development

Early exposure to business concepts and opportunities creates long-term community capacity.

Implementation strategy:

- Develop age-appropriate entrepreneurship curricula
- Create youth business incubation programs with real-world application
- Establish mentorship connections between youth and active entrepreneurs
- Implement business plan competitions with implementation support
- Create internship pathways into community businesses

For James, an attorney we advised, strategic mentorship became his primary community contribution. He established a legal mentorship program specifically for small business owners, providing guidance on entity selection, contract development, intellectual property protection, and other critical legal matters. The program combined workshop education, one-on-one consultation, and standardized document templates, making essential legal knowledge accessible to emerging entrepreneurs.

"As an attorney, I saw how lack of legal knowledge created unnecessary barriers for talented entrepreneurs," James explained. "By creating a structured knowledge transfer program rather than just occasional advice, I could help dozens of businesses simultaneously while still maintaining my own practice. The collective impact has far exceeded what I could have achieved through traditional pro bono service."

The Ripple Effect of Family Wealth on Community Prosperity

When families build sustainable wealth using the principles outlined throughout The Abundance Formula, their impact naturally extends beyond immediate family boundaries. Understanding and intentionally amplifying these ripple effects creates substantial community benefit.

Key Ripple Effect Mechanisms

Several specific pathways translate family wealth into community prosperity:

1. Employment Creation

Family businesses and investment activities create employment opportunities with community impact beyond just wages.

Implementation strategy:

- Prioritize hiring from within the community when possible
- Develop training programs addressing skills gaps
- Implement wage and benefit approaches supporting family stability
- Create career advancement pathways rather than just entry-level positions
- Design scheduling and support systems addressing community-specific needs

2. Physical Infrastructure Development

Investment in community physical infrastructure creates benefits extended well beyond financial returns.

Implementation strategy:

- Focus real estate investment in underserved areas with growth potential
- Prioritize developments addressing community-identified needs
- Implement design approaches that enhance neighborhood quality and safety
- Create mixed-use developments supporting business and residential needs
- Establish maintenance and enhancement standards that protect long-term value

3. Financial Education Proliferation

Knowledge shared beyond family boundaries creates exponential impact.

Implementation strategy:

- Develop accessible financial education curricula for various knowledge levels
- Create peer-based learning communities with implementation support
- Establish ongoing support systems sustaining behavior change
- Implement "train the trainer" approaches multiplying educational impact
- Create recognition systems celebrating financial capability development

4. Community Cultural Capital Enhancement

Investment in cultural institutions and expressions strengthens community identity and cohesion.

Implementation strategy:

- Support arts organizations with community representation and focus
- Develop cultural assets with both community and economic value
- Create physical spaces supporting cultural expression and celebration

CHAPTER 10: EMPOWERING THE COMMUNITY

- Implement programs documenting and preserving community heritage
- Establish sustainable business models for cultural programming

5. Next-Generation Leadership Development

Youth leadership development creates long-term community capability.

Implementation strategy:

- Create structured programs identifying and nurturing leadership potential
- Develop mentorship pairings with established community leaders
- Implement project-based learning addressing real community challenges
- Establish academic support ensuring educational achievement
- Create recognizable pathways connecting youth leadership to adult roles

For the Thompson family we advised, understanding these ripple effects transformed their approach to wealth building. Beyond creating their family real estate portfolio, they established a focused strategy for neighborhood revitalization—purchasing and renovating commercial properties in a historically significant but underinvested area, creating affordable spaces for Black-owned businesses while enhancing neighborhood infrastructure and appearance.

"We realized our real estate investments could achieve multiple objectives simultaneously," Mrs. Thompson explained. "By focusing our portfolio in a specific neighborhood with historical significance, we could generate financial returns while helping revitalize an area tied to our community's heritage. The investment performs well financially while creating space for new businesses, preserving architectural character, and generating neighborhood pride."

Practicing Group Economics: Strategic Implementation

Moving from conceptual understanding to practical implementation requires strategic approaches adapted to your specific capabilities, resources, and community context.

The Group Economics Implementation Spectrum

Effective implementation typically progresses through several stages of increasing commitment and impact:

Stage 1: Intentional Consumption (Entry Level)

Redirect existing spending to support community economic development.

Implementation steps:

1. Audit current spending across major categories
2. Research Black-owned alternatives in each category
3. Create a prioritized transition plan based on impact and accessibility

4. Establish personal accountability systems for spending goals
5. Track and celebrate spending shifts with measurable metrics

Stage 2: Active Promotion (Intermediate Level)

Leverage personal and professional networks to expand support beyond direct spending.

Implementation steps:

1. Identify businesses aligned with network needs and interests
2. Develop concise, compelling introductions and recommendations
3. Create facilitated introduction systems rather than passive referrals
4. Establish reciprocal value creation rather than unidirectional support
5. Implement feedback systems improving business/customer alignment

Stage 3: Strategic Investment (Advanced Level)

Deploy capital to strengthen business and community infrastructure.

Implementation steps:

1. Define investment criteria balancing financial and community returns
2. Develop appropriate investment vehicles for objectives

3. Create due diligence processes addressing unique community business factors
4. Implement post-investment support systems enhancing success probability
5. Establish measurement systems tracking both financial and community impact

Stage 4: Ecosystem Development (Leadership Level)

Create coordinated systems addressing multiple community economic needs simultaneously.

Implementation steps:

1. Conduct community economic ecosystem assessment identifying gaps and assets
2. Develop strategic plan addressing highest-leverage intervention points
3. Create collaborative structures engaging multiple stakeholders
4. Implement coordinated initiatives with unified measurement systems
5. Establish sustainable governance ensuring long-term system functionality

Stage 5: Institutional Development (Legacy Level)

Build enduring institutions that outlast individual involvement while addressing structural barriers.

Implementation steps:

1. Identify institutional gaps limiting community economic development
2. Create governance and operational models ensuring institutional durability
3. Develop sustainable funding mechanisms supporting core functions
4. Implement leadership development ensuring generational transition
5. Establish partnerships enhancing institutional effectiveness and reach

Implementation Optimization Strategies

Regardless of implementation stage, several strategies enhance effectiveness:

1. Collaborative Approaches

Partnering with others multiplies impact while distributing effort.

Implementation principles:

- Identify potential collaborators with complementary resources and capabilities
- Develop clear partnership agreements establishing expectations and commitments
- Create governance structures appropriate to initiative scale and complexity

- Implement transparent communication preventing misunderstandings
- Establish fair recognition systems acknowledging all contributions

2. Leverage Optimization

Strategic use of your specific capabilities creates outsized impact relative to resources invested.

Implementation principles:

- Identify your unique skills, relationships, and resources
- Focus initiatives where your specific advantages create maximum leverage
- Develop systems multiplying impact beyond direct involvement
- Implement technology and standardization creating efficiency
- Create measurement focusing efforts on highest-impact activities

3. Sustainable Design

Building sustainability from inception prevents initiative abandonment after initial enthusiasm fades.

Implementation principles:

- Create viable economic models rather than perpetual subsidy requirements
- Develop leadership depth preventing single-person dependence

- Implement documentation supporting knowledge transfer
- Establish realistic resource requirements matched to available commitments
- Create milestone-based evaluation preventing mission drift

For Marcus, implementing these strategies transformed both his impact and satisfaction. He progressed from initially redirecting his personal spending to Black-owned businesses (Stage 1) to eventually establishing a community development financial institution (CDFI) providing capital, technical assistance, and market connections to entrepreneurs in his childhood neighborhood (Stage 5).

"I realized I needed to match my implementation to both my capabilities and the community's needs," Marcus reflected. "By starting with manageable steps and progressing strategically, I avoided both overwhelm and ineffectiveness. Each stage built on the previous one, creating momentum that attracted additional partners and resources."

Building Economic Bridges Beyond the Community

While focused community economic development forms the foundation of group economics, building strategic connections to broader economic systems creates additional opportunities for sustainable prosperity.

Strategic Bridge-Building Approaches

Several specific connection points create valuable economic linkages:

1. Corporate Partnership Programs

Structured engagement with larger corporations creates both market access and resource connection.

Implementation strategy:

- Identify corporations with relevant supply chain or market opportunities
- Develop capability assessment determining readiness for corporate engagement
- Create preparation programs addressing identified capability gaps
- Implement introduction systems beyond traditional networking events
- Establish performance feedback loops supporting continuous improvement

2. Inter-Community Economic Alliances

Strategic connections between different community economic ecosystems create mutual benefits.

Implementation strategy:

- Identify complementary strengths and needs between communities
- Develop formal or informal trade agreements establishing expectations
- Create connector roles facilitating ongoing exchange
- Implement cultural bridge-building supporting economic relationships
- Establish conflict resolution mechanisms maintaining relationship health

3. Global Diaspora Connections

Relationships with African diaspora communities worldwide create unique opportunities.

Implementation strategy:

- Identify diaspora communities with complementary economic assets
- Develop cultural understanding supporting effective engagement
- Create specific trade or investment opportunities with mutual benefit
- Implement technology supporting distance collaboration
- Establish long-term relationship nurturing beyond transactional exchange

4. Industry Sector Development

Strategic focus on specific industry sectors creates specialized expertise and recognition.

Implementation strategy:

- Identify sectors with both community capability alignment and growth potential
- Develop specialized education creating sector-specific workforce capability
- Create business clusters establishing sector identity and credibility
- Implement marketing communicating sector strengths to external markets
- Establish continuous innovation maintaining competitive advantage

5. Economic Policy Engagement

Strategic involvement in economic policy development creates structural opportunity expansion.

Implementation strategy:

- Identify policy areas with significant community economic impact
- Develop data-driven policy analysis supporting effective advocacy
- Create coalition relationships enhancing influence

- Implement balanced approaches addressing both policy change and utilization
- Establish ongoing monitoring ensuring implementation and impact

For Jason, a technology entrepreneur we advised, strategic bridge-building transformed his business from a small community-focused enterprise to an international company while maintaining strong community roots. He initially built his software development business serving local clients, then established a strategic partnership with a global technology firm seeking to diversify its supplier base. This partnership provided access to larger contracts while creating local employment in a high-growth sector.

"Building bridges beyond our immediate community created opportunities I couldn't have accessed otherwise," Jason noted. "The key was approaching these relationships from a position of value creation rather than charity-seeking. By thoroughly understanding what we uniquely offered, we could establish partnerships benefiting both sides while remaining rooted in our community mission."

The Balanced Approach: Personal Success and Community Responsibility

Effective community economic empowerment requires balancing personal wealth building with community contribution—neither sacrificing individual prosperity nor isolating success from community impact.

The Integrated Prosperity Framework

This balanced approach integrates personal and community success through several key principles:

1. Strength-Based Contribution

Leverage personal success to create meaningful community impact aligned with your specific capabilities.

Implementation approach:

- Build substantial personal financial foundation creating contribution capacity
- Identify unique skills, resources, and relationships you can leverage
- Focus community efforts where your specific strengths create maximum impact
- Develop sustainable contribution approaches preventing burnout
- Create measurement systems evaluating both personal and community outcomes

2. Progressive Engagement

Scale community involvement appropriately as personal capacity increases.

Implementation approach:

- Begin with manageable community commitments during wealth-building phase
- Increase engagement strategically as financial foundation strengthens
- Develop clear decision criteria for balancing personal and community investment
- Implement periodic reassessment ensuring alignment with evolving capacity
- Create legacy structures continuing impact beyond personal involvement

3. Mission-Aligned Opportunities

Seek wealth-building opportunities that simultaneously advance community prosperity.

Implementation approach:

- Identify investment sectors with both personal return and community benefit
- Develop evaluation criteria measuring dual-bottom-line performance
- Create investment structures appropriately balancing financial and social returns
- Implement hybrid approaches capturing both market and mission value
- Establish measurement systems tracking integrated performance

4. Strategic Resource Leverage

Amplify impact by catalyzing additional resources beyond personal contribution.

Implementation approach:

- Use personal resources to attract additional capital through partnerships
- Develop demonstration projects establishing concept viability
- Create scaling systems extending impact beyond direct involvement
- Implement knowledge transfer multiplying capability development
- Establish leadership development ensuring initiative sustainability

5. Reciprocal Benefit Recognition

Acknowledge that community prosperity creates substantial personal benefits beyond altruism.

Implementation approach:

- Identify specific ways community strength enhances personal opportunity
- Develop measurement capturing reciprocal value creation
- Create communication highlighting mutual benefit rather than charity
- Implement celebration recognizing all forms of contribution

- Establish mentorship communicating integrated prosperity principles

For Danielle, a physician we advised, implementing the integrated prosperity framework transformed both her financial trajectory and community impact. While building her medical practice and personal investment portfolio, she established a strategic community initiative focused on healthcare workforce development—creating scholarships, mentorship, and internship opportunities for promising students from underrepresented backgrounds interested in healthcare careers.

"I realized I didn't have to choose between personal financial success and community contribution," Danielle explained. "By developing an approach that leveraged my specific knowledge, relationships, and resources in the healthcare field, I could create significant impact while still building my practice and investments. The reciprocal benefits have been remarkable—the program graduates now include colleagues, employees, and even potential practice purchasers as I approach retirement."

Marcus: Four Years Later

Let's revisit Marcus's journey four years after implementing his community empowerment strategy alongside his personal wealth building.

His transformation has been remarkable:

Community Investment Development:

- Established a commercial real estate investment focus in his childhood neighborhood

- Created a business incubator providing affordable space for local entrepreneurs
- Developed a private investment fund focusing on community businesses
- Implemented a structured mentorship program for emerging technology entrepreneurs
- Established a coding education program creating tech workforce capability

Professional Evolution:

- Leveraged community technology focus to develop new professional expertise
- Created consulting practice focused on technology implementation in underserved markets
- Built professional network including both community entrepreneurs and corporate partners
- Developed reputation as thought leader in inclusive technology development
- Created speaking and writing platform sharing community economic development approach

Personal Wealth Expansion:

- Found his community-focused real estate investments outperformed broader market
- Discovered unique investment opportunities through community engagement
- Built valuable relationships enhancing career and business opportunities

- Developed new skills through community work transferable to professional advancement
- Created tax advantages through strategic community investment structures

Personal Fulfillment Enhancement:

- Found deeper purpose and meaning in integrated success approach
- Built relationships across traditional community boundaries
- Discovered intellectual stimulation in community economic challenges
- Created legacy extending beyond personal financial achievement
- Developed leadership bringing new dimensions to personal capability

"What started as feeling something was missing in my success has become the most fulfilling aspect of my life," Marcus reflected. "The surprising discovery was how community empowerment actually accelerated my personal wealth building rather than diminishing it. The opportunities, relationships, and knowledge I've gained through community engagement have created financial returns I wouldn't have accessed otherwise, while giving my success deeper purpose and meaning."

Your Community Empowerment Journey

As we conclude this final chapter of The Abundance Formula, remember that true abundance extends beyond personal financial achievement to create prosperity that lifts entire communities. When implemented alongside the nine previous components, community empowerment completes the virtuous cycle—creating an environment where wealth-building knowledge, opportunity, and support become widely available, benefiting both individuals and the collective.

Whether you're just beginning to consider community economic engagement or looking to enhance existing initiatives, the principles in this chapter provide a framework for creating impact aligned with your specific capabilities and resources. Start where you are, implement approaches matched to your current capacity, and remember that collective prosperity ultimately creates the most sustainable foundation for individual success.

For Black families building generational wealth, community economic empowerment takes on particular significance. Given historical barriers to wealth creation and the continuing challenges of economic inequality, isolated individual success remains vulnerable to systemic limitations. By implementing the group economics approaches outlined in this chapter alongside personal wealth building, we create both individual financial security and the collective economic strength necessary to address structural barriers while creating opportunity ecosystems benefiting current and future generations.

As you implement your own integrated prosperity approach, remember Marcus's journey—from successful yet incomplete individual achievement to the deeper fulfillment and expanded opportunity of integrated personal and community prosperity. With strategic implementation, your wealth-building journey can create ripples extending far beyond your immediate family, establishing a legacy of abundance that strengthens and empowers your broader community for generations to come.

CHAPTER 10: EMPOWERING THE COMMUNITY

ACTION STEP: Identify Ways to Contribute to Your Community's Economic Empowerment

- **Assess your current community economic engagement**
    - Inventory your current community-focused activities and contributions
    - Evaluate alignment between your specific capabilities and community needs
    - Identify gaps between your wealth-building activities and community engagement
    - Calculate the percentage of your spending supporting community businesses
    - Assess your knowledge sharing beyond immediate family circles
- **Clarify your community empowerment objectives**
    - Define the specific community or communities you wish to impact
    - Identify economic areas where you have particular expertise or resources
    - Determine your available time, financial, and relationship resources
    - Clarify your personal motivation for community economic engagement
    - Define what success would look like for both community and personal outcomes

- **Select appropriate implementation approaches**
  - Identify your current position on the implementation spectrum (Stages 1-5)
  - Select initial activities aligned with your capacity and community needs
  - Develop specific metrics for measuring both input and impact
  - Create a progressive engagement plan as capacity increases
  - Identify potential collaborators with complementary capabilities
- **Design your engagement implementation system**
  - Schedule specific action steps with deadlines
  - Establish reflection points for assessing impact and adjustment
  - Create accountability systems maintaining commitment
  - Develop knowledge acquisition addressing capability gaps
  - Establish celebration recognizing both personal and community achievement
- **Implement first-stage engagement activities**
  - Execute initial commitment regardless of scale
  - Document both process insights and outcomes
  - Share experiences with others to multiply impact
  - Evaluate results against expectations
  - Begin planning next-stage engagement

Remember: Effective community economic empowerment begins with understanding your unique capabilities and matching them with specific

CHAPTER 10: EMPOWERING THE COMMUNITY

community needs. The most sustainable approach balances personal financial strength with strategic community contribution, creating integrated prosperity that benefits both individual families and the broader community ecosystem.

CONCLUSION

LIVING THE ABUNDANCE FORMULA

"We are not just the owners of our abundance, but stewards of it for future generations."
—Ash Cash and Amina Phelps

Throughout this book, we've walked together through the nine proven steps of The Abundance Formula—a comprehensive system for building sustainable wealth for Black families. We've explored everything from aligning your spending with your values to establishing your legacy for future generations. As we conclude our journey together, let's reflect on how these principles come together to create a life of true abundance.

The Integrated Abundance Approach

The power of The Abundance Formula lies not in any single component but in their integration into a cohesive wealth-building system. When implemented together, these nine steps create a virtuous cycle:

1. **A**lign Your Savings and Spending: Creating the foundation for wealth by ensuring money flows toward priorities
2. **B**roaden Your Earnings: Developing multiple income streams for both security and growth
3. **U**nderwrite Your Financial Freedom Fund: Building the safety that enables strategic risk-taking
4. **N**urture Creditworthiness: Transforming credit from a consumer tool to a wealth-building leverage system
5. **D**iminish Liabilities: Eliminating wealth-draining debt while strategically using good debt
6. **A**mplify Investments: Converting savings into growth vehicles across multiple asset classes
7. **N**avigate a Life Insurance Strategy: Building protection, tax advantages, and wealth transfer efficiency
8. **C**reate a Tax Wealth Strategy: Keeping more of what you earn through strategic planning
9. **E**stablish Legacy: Ensuring your wealth empowers rather than hinders future generations
10. **Empower the Community:** Extending prosperity beyond your family to strengthen collective wealth

Each step builds upon the previous ones, creating a comprehensive approach addressing both the technical aspects of wealth building and the psychological, familial, and community dimensions that give wealth its true purpose and meaning.

CONCLUSION: LIVING THE ABUNDANCE FORMULA

Beyond the Formula: The Abundance Mindset

While the strategic components of The Abundance Formula provide the practical framework for wealth building, implementing them successfully requires developing what we call the Abundance Mindset—a way of thinking about wealth that differs fundamentally from typical financial perspectives.

Key Elements of the Abundance Mindset

1. Stewardship vs. Ownership

The Abundance Mindset views wealth not as something we possess solely for ourselves, but as resources we steward for family, community, and future generations. This perspective shifts our relationship with wealth from consumption-focused to legacy-focused.

2. Collaboration vs. Competition

Rather than seeing economic life as a zero-sum competition where some must lose for others to win, the Abundance Mindset recognizes that collaborative approaches often create greater prosperity for all participants. This fosters strategic partnerships rather than isolated striving.

3. Long-Term vs. Short-Term Thinking

The Abundance Mindset extends the time horizon for decision-making from immediate gratification to multigenerational impact. This perspective transforms how we evaluate options and opportunities, prioritizing sustainable growth over quick wins.

4. **Value Creation vs. Value Extraction**

Instead of focusing primarily on extracting value from existing systems, the Abundance Mindset emphasizes creating new value through innovation, service, and problem-solving. This naturally expands available prosperity rather than merely redistributing it.

5. **Possibility vs. Scarcity Orientation**

Where scarcity thinking focuses on limitations and constraints, the Abundance Mindset remains attuned to possibilities and opportunities. This doesn't ignore real challenges but approaches them as problems to be solved rather than permanent barriers.

Cultivating these mindset elements doesn't happen overnight—it's a gradual process of shifting perspective as you implement the practical steps of The Abundance Formula. Over time, these ways of thinking become increasingly natural, informing not just financial decisions but your entire approach to life and legacy.

The Journey Beyond This Book

As you implement The Abundance Formula in your own life, remember that wealth building is not a destination but a journey—one that unfolds over years and decades rather than days or months. Here are some principles to guide your path forward:

1. Progress Over Perfection

Focus on consistent implementation rather than flawless execution. Small steps taken regularly create more progress than perfect plans never acted upon. Celebrate incremental improvements while maintaining vision for the ultimate goal.

2. Personalization Over Prescription

While The Abundance Formula provides a proven framework, your implementation should reflect your unique circumstances, values, and objectives. Adapt the principles to your specific situation rather than forcing rigid adherence to any particular approach.

3. Process Over Outcomes

While ultimate outcomes matter, focusing excessively on results creates both anxiety and impatience. Instead, concentrate on mastering the processes that naturally produce desired outcomes over time. The wealth-building journey becomes more sustainable when we find satisfaction in the daily and weekly practices themselves.

4. Community Over Isolation

Seeking community with others on similar journeys provides both practical wisdom and emotional support. Consider forming or joining wealth-building mastermind groups, finding knowledgeable mentors, or creating accountability partnerships to strengthen your implementation.

5. Education as Ongoing Investment

View continued financial education as a crucial investment rather than an optional extra. The financial landscape constantly evolves, creating both new opportunities and challenges. Commit to regular learning through books, courses, trusted advisors, and practical experience.

6. Reflection as Strategic Tool

Schedule regular reflection points to assess your progress, identify adjustments needed, and reconnect with your deeper purposes for wealth building. These reflection periods—whether quarterly, semi-annually, or annually—prevent drift from your intended path while providing opportunities to celebrate progress.

7. Balance as Sustainable Approach

Maintain balance between building wealth and enjoying life along the journey. The most sustainable wealth-building approaches integrate with a fulfilling lifestyle rather than demanding complete sacrifice of present satisfaction for future goals.

CONCLUSION: LIVING THE ABUNDANCE FORMULA

A Vision of Abundance Realized

As you implement The Abundance Formula consistently over time, what might the resulting life of abundance look like? While specific details vary based on individual values and circumstances, certain common elements typically emerge:

Financial Sovereignty: Freedom from financial anxiety, with sufficient reserves, income streams, and assets to weather challenges while pursuing opportunities without desperation or fear.

Purpose-Aligned Resources: Wealth structured to support what matters most to you—whether family security, community impact, creative pursuits, or other deeply held values.

Knowledge Transferability: Financial wisdom continuously shared across generations, building capability rather than just transferring assets.

Strategic Flexibility: Adaptability to changing circumstances without fundamental financial disruption, maintaining core security amid evolving conditions.

Community Connection: Meaningful engagement with broader community prosperity rather than isolated individual success, creating value circles extending beyond immediate family.

Legacy Confirmation: Confidence that your wealth will continue producing positive impact beyond your lifetime, supporting your deepest values and priorities through future generations.

Present Appreciation: Ability to enjoy current abundance while continuing to build future prosperity, without excessive anxiety about either present spending or future security.

This vision isn't about specific dollar amounts or particular lifestyle elements. Rather, it represents a state of alignment between your resources and your most deeply held values—a life where money serves as a tool for expressing what matters most rather than becoming an end in itself or a source of persistent worry.

Your Invitation

As we reach the conclusion of this book, we extend an invitation to join us and countless others implementing The Abundance Formula to transform not just individual financial realities but the broader economic landscape of our communities.

The historical wealth gap affecting Black Americans didn't arise by accident, nor will it be eliminated without intentional, strategic action. By implementing these nine proven steps consistently over time, you position yourself and your family to overcome historical barriers while creating new pathways of opportunity that can extend for generations.

More than this, as you achieve increasing financial success using these principles, you gain the capacity to reach back and lift others—sharing knowledge, creating opportunity, building infrastructure, and strengthening community prosperity. This expanding circle of abundance represents perhaps the most powerful aspect of the Formula: its ability to create not just individual wealth but collective advancement.

We invite you to begin—or continue—your abundance journey today. Whether implementing your first financial freedom fund, establishing your initial additional income stream, or refining advanced wealth transfer strategies, take one concrete step forward on your path to abundance.

We've provided the Formula. The application now rests in your capable hands.

With abundant blessings on your journey,

Ash Cash & Amina Phelps

APPENDICES

APPENDIX 1: The Abundance Checklist Worksheet

Use this comprehensive checklist to track your progress implementing The Abundance Formula in your financial life. Check each item as you complete it, creating a visual record of your wealth-building journey.

Step 1: Align Your Savings and Spending

Financial Foundation:

- ☐ Created personal financial statement (net worth and cash flow)
- ☐ Established SMART financial goals (short, medium, and long-term)
- ☐ Implemented "pay yourself first" automatic savings system
- ☐ Developed spending plan aligned with core values
- ☐ Established regular financial review schedule

Advanced Implementation:

- ☐ Created separate accounts for different financial purposes
- ☐ Implemented zero-based or percentage-based budgeting system

- [ ] Developed strategies for managing irregular expenses
- [ ] Established accountability system for financial goals
- [ ] Created celebration milestones for financial achievements

Step 2: Broaden Your Earnings

Primary Income Optimization:

- [ ] Evaluated current career path for growth potential
- [ ] Identified skills development to increase earning capacity
- [ ] Implemented strategic advancement plan in current field
- [ ] Developed negotiation strategy for compensation
- [ ] Created performance measurement demonstrating value

Additional Income Streams:

- [ ] Identified potential supplementary income sources
- [ ] Established first additional income stream
- [ ] Developed system for managing multiple income sources
- [ ] Created plan for income stream expansion
- [ ] Implemented tax strategy for multiple income streams

Step 3: Underwrite Your Financial Freedom Fund

Emergency Fund Establishment:

- [ ] Calculated optimal freedom fund target amount
- [ ] Established dedicated freedom fund account(s)
- [ ] Implemented automatic contribution system

- ☐ Developed clear guidelines for appropriate fund use
- ☐ Created replenishment strategy for after fund use

Freedom Fund Optimization:

- ☐ Implemented tiered liquidity structure for different needs
- ☐ Optimized interest/return on fund while maintaining safety
- ☐ Created regular review system for fund adequacy
- ☐ Developed inflation adjustment strategy for fund target
- ☐ Established clear separation between freedom fund and investments

Step 4: Nurture Creditworthiness

Credit Foundation:

- ☐ Obtained and reviewed credit reports from all three bureaus
- ☐ Disputed any inaccuracies on credit reports
- ☐ Established on-time payment systems for all obligations
- ☐ Implemented strategy to reduce credit utilization
- ☐ Developed appropriate credit mix

Strategic Credit Use:

- ☐ Established optimal credit structures for wealth building
- ☐ Implemented credit monitoring system
- ☐ Developed strategic approach to credit applications
- ☐ Created plan for leveraging credit for investment opportunities
- ☐ Established clear guidelines for appropriate credit use

Step 5: Diminish Liabilities

Debt Reduction:

- ☐ Categorized all debt as good, bad, or neutral
- ☐ Developed strategic debt elimination plan
- ☐ Implemented accelerated payoff strategy for high-interest debt
- ☐ Established debt prevention systems
- ☐ Created celebration milestones for debt reduction achievement

Strategic Borrowing:

- ☐ Identified appropriate uses of good debt for wealth building
- ☐ Implemented favorable debt restructuring where beneficial
- ☐ Established systems for evaluating borrowing opportunities
- ☐ Developed clear risk management guidelines for leveraged investments
- ☐ Created strategic borrowing opportunity fund

Step 6: Amplify Investments

Investment Foundation:

- ☐ Established investment philosophy and approach
- ☐ Created strategic asset allocation aligned with goals
- ☐ Implemented regular investment contribution system
- ☐ Developed investment policy statement
- ☐ Established appropriate investment accounts (retirement and taxable)

Advanced Investment Strategy:

- ☐ Implemented tax-efficient investment placement strategy
- ☐ Established regular rebalancing system
- ☐ Developed investment opportunity fund
- ☐ Created system for investment performance measurement
- ☐ Established investment learning curriculum for ongoing education

Step 7: Navigate a Life Insurance Strategy

Protection Foundation:

- ☐ Calculated appropriate life insurance coverage needs
- ☐ Obtained adequate term life insurance
- ☐ Evaluated disability and other protection needs
- ☐ Established regular insurance review schedule
- ☐ Created clear beneficiary designation strategy

Advanced Insurance Strategies:

- ☐ Evaluated strategic permanent insurance opportunities
- ☐ Implemented appropriate trust ownership for insurance
- ☐ Developed insurance-based wealth transfer strategy
- ☐ Created family banking system using insurance
- ☐ Established coordination between insurance and overall financial plan

Step 8: Create a Tax Wealth Strategy

Tax Planning Foundation:

- ☐ Established relationship with tax planning professional
- ☐ Implemented tax projection system
- ☐ Developed tax documentation organization system
- ☐ Created strategic income timing approach
- ☐ Established regular tax planning meeting schedule

Advanced Tax Strategies:

- ☐ Implemented appropriate business structures for tax advantage
- ☐ Developed real estate tax strategy
- ☐ Created retirement account tax diversification strategy
- ☐ Implemented strategic charitable giving approach
- ☐ Established multi-year tax optimization plan

Step 9: Establish Legacy

Estate Planning Foundation:

- ☐ Created or updated will
- ☐ Established advance directives and powers of attorney
- ☐ Developed guardianship plan for minor children
- ☐ Created asset inventory and access information
- ☐ Communicated basic plans to appropriate family members

Advanced Legacy Planning:

- ☐ Established appropriate trust structures
- ☐ Developed family wealth mission statement
- ☐ Created financial education system for heirs
- ☐ Implemented family governance structure
- ☐ Established legacy letter or ethical will

Step 10: Empower the Community

Community Support Foundation:

- ☐ Evaluated current community economic engagement
- ☐ Identified strategic community support opportunities aligned with capabilities
- ☐ Implemented intentional spending with community businesses
- ☐ Developed knowledge sharing approach for community benefit
- ☐ Created measurement system for community impact

Advanced Community Empowerment:

- ☐ Established strategic investment in community development
- ☐ Developed mentorship program for community entrepreneurs
- ☐ Created community-focused investment vehicle
- ☐ Implemented collaborative community economic initiative
- ☐ Established family tradition of community economic engagement

Appendix 2: Resources For Financial Literacy

Books

Foundational Financial Education:

- *"Financial Literacy for All"* by John Hope Bryant
- *"You Deserve to Be Rich"* by Rashad Bilal & Troy Millings
- *"Get Good with Money"* by Tiffany Aliche
- *"The Wealth Choice"* by Dr. Dennis Kimbro
- *"Rich and Righteous"* by Jullien Gordon
- Any Book by Ash Cash Exantus (Start w/ Hip-Hoponomics Series)

Black Economic Empowerment:

- *"PowerNomics"* by Dr. Claud Anderson
- *"Black Wealth/White Wealth"* by Melvin Oliver and Thomas Shapiro
- *"The Black Tax"* by Shawn Rochester
- *"The Color of Money"* by Mehrsa Baradaran
- *"Our Black Year"* by Maggie Anderson

Advanced Wealth Strategies:

- *"What Would the Rockefellers Do?"* by Garrett Gunderson
- *"Family Wealth"* by James E. Hughes Jr.
- *"Die with Zero"* by Bill Perkins
- *"Tax-Free Wealth"* by Tom Wheelwright
- *"Becoming Your Own Banker"* by R. Nelson Nash

Online Learning Resources

Free Courses and Education:

- Khan Academy Personal Finance (www.khanacademy.org/college-careers-more/personal-finance)
- Coursera Personal & Family Financial Planning (www.coursera.org/learn/family-planning)
- edX Personal Finance (www.edx.org/learn/personal-finance)
- Consumer Financial Protection Bureau Resources (www.consumerfinance.gov/consumer-tools)
- Federal Reserve Economic Education (www.federalreserveeducation.org)

Paid Programs and Memberships:

- Join The Abundance Community

  ♀ www.TheAbundanceCommunity.com

  If you're ready to take control of your finances, build real wealth, and secure your family's financial future, JOIN THE ABUNDANCE COMMUNITY today!

  The Abundance Community is a premium membership program designed to help you implement The Abundance Formula—a proven 9-step blueprint to create financial independence, protect your legacy, and empower generations.

  This isn't just a course. It's a movement. It's a community of like-minded wealth-builders dedicated to financial freedom, no matter what's happening in politics, the economy, or the job market. When you join, you'll gain access to everything you need to win financially—with guidance, tools, and direct mentorship to help you apply these strategies in your own life.

What You Get When You Join The Abundance Community:

☑ **Live Weekly Coaching & Office Hours**

✔ Get direct access to Ash Cash and expert mentors for Q&A, real-time coaching, and strategic financial planning.

☑ **Step-by-Step Wealth-Building Courses**

✔ Learn how to align your finances, increase your income, eliminate debt, invest smartly, and create generational wealth using The Abundance Formula.

☑ **Exclusive Investment & Business Strategies**

✔ Get insider access to real estate investing, stock market strategies, business growth blueprints, and tax-saving secrets that the wealthy use to build and maintain their empires.

☑ **Private Members-Only Community**

✔ Connect with entrepreneurs, investors, and financial experts all committed to wealth-building, networking, and group economics.

☑ **Financial Tools, Templates & Resources**

✔ Download budgeting templates, credit repair guides, investment calculators, business funding checklists, and more to make wealth-building effortless.

☑ **Special Wealth Challenges & Action Plans**

✔ Participate in financial growth challenges, passive income blueprints, and accountability programs to keep you focused and on track.

☑ **VIP Discounts on Coaching & Wealth Events**

✔ Get priority access and exclusive discounts to masterminds, wealth-building retreats, and live events where you can learn directly from experts.

Why You Should Join The Abundance Community

💰 Because Wealth Is Built WITH People – Surround yourself with winners who are serious about financial freedom.

🧮 Because Knowledge Without Action Is Useless – This isn't just about learning—it's about executing and seeing real results.

🏛 Because No One's Coming to Save Us – If you don't take control of your finances NOW, who will?

🚀 Join The Abundance Community Today!

💧 Membership starts at just $44/month. 💧

📍 Visit 👉 www.TheAbundanceCommunity.com

○ Get instant access to wealth-building strategies, live coaching, and an entire community ready to support your success!

Your path to financial freedom, generational wealth, and true economic power starts NOW. Join The Abundance Community today!

Podcasts

Personal Finance:

- "The Ash Cash Show"
- "Inside the Vault w/ Ash Cash"
- "Abundance Conversations w/ Ash Cash & Amina Phelps"
- "Trappin' Tuesday's w/ WallStreet Trapper"
- "Market Monday's w/ Ian Dunlap and Earn Your Leisure"

Black Finance and Wealth Building:

- "The Dr. Boyce Breakdown"
- "Side Hustle Pro"
- "Brown Ambition"
- "Money on the Table"
- "The His & Her Money Show"

Advanced Wealth Strategies:

- "Wealth Formula"
- "Wealth Matters"
- "The Estate Planning Guy"

- "Real Estate Investing for Cash Flow"
- "Tax-Free Wealth"

Apps and Tools

Budgeting and Expense Tracking:

- The Abundance Calculator
- Mint
- YNAB (You Need A Budget)
- Personal Capital
- EveryDollar
- Goodbudget

Investing and Wealth Building:

- Robinhood
- M1 Finance
- Stash
- Acorns
- Public

Financial Education:

- Hip-Hoponomics
- Investopedia
- Money Prodigy
- Financial Diet

Community Resources

Professional Organizations:

- Association for Financial Counseling & Planning Education (AFCPE)
- National Association of Personal Financial Advisors (NAPFA)
- Financial Planning Association (FPA)
- Society for Financial Education & Professional Development
- Association of African American Financial Advisors

Community Development Organizations:

- National Urban League Economic Empowerment Programs
- Operation HOPE Financial Dignity Centers
- Black Wealth 2020
- Community Development Financial Institutions (CDFIs)
- Local Small Business Development Centers

APPENDIX 3: Family Wealth Planning Templates

Family Wealth Mission Statement Template

Use this template to develop your family's wealth mission statement, identifying core values, priorities, and intentions for your financial resources.

1. Family Values Identification

List 5-7 core values that guide your family's relationship with wealth:

1.
2.
3.
4.
5.
6.
7.

2. Wealth Purpose Definition

Complete the following statements:

- Our family's financial resources exist primarily to: _____

  _____

  _____

- The most important outcomes we want our wealth to create are: _____

  _____

- We define "enough" as: _____

  _____

  _____

- We believe wealth should be used to: _____

  _____

  _____

- The relationship between wealth and happiness for our family is: _____

  _____

3. Legacy Vision Articulation

Describe your vision for how your wealth will impact:

- Future generations of your family: _____

  _____

  _____

- Your community: _____

_____

_____

- Causes or issues important to you: _____

_____

_____

Indicate your intended timeframe for wealth impact:

- Current generation primarily _____
- Children and grandchildren _____
- Multiple generations (3+) _____
- Perpetual/Enduring _____

4. Wealth Governance Principles

Define how wealth decisions should be made:

- Who should participate in wealth decisions: _____

_____

_____

- How conflicts about wealth should be resolved: _____

_____

_____

- The balance between individual autonomy and family cohesion:

  _____

  _____

- The role of professional advisors: _____

  _____

  _____

- How wealth information should be shared within the family: __

  _____

  _____

5. Final Mission Statement

Based on the above elements, draft your complete family wealth mission statement (typically 100-250 words):

_____

_____

_____

_____

Below is an example of Our Family Wealth Mission Statement:

Exantus-Phelps Family Wealth Mission Statement

We, **Ash Cash Exantus** and **Amina Phelps**, believe that wealth is not just about money—it is about purpose, power, and legacy. Our financial resources exist to create generational freedom, promote unity within our family, and empower the communities we serve. We are committed to building, protecting, and circulating wealth in alignment with our faith, values, and the belief that **Abundance is our birthright**.

Our wealth is a tool to **educate, uplift, and inspire**. It exists to ensure that our children—and their children's children—never have to start from zero. We define "enough" not by a dollar amount, but by our ability to live in alignment with our divine calling, free from financial stress, while creating opportunities for others to thrive.

Our mission is to use our wealth to impact our **family**, our **community**, and the **world**. We are dedicated to investing in education, entrepreneurship, financial literacy, and legacy planning. We will use our resources to support causes close to our hearts, including Black empowerment, autism awareness, and the self-education of Black children and families.

All wealth decisions will be made with **transparency, wisdom, and integrity**. We will work together as a unified family to uphold these values, guided by trusted advisors and grounded in love. Our goal is not just to leave an inheritance, but to leave instructions, principles, and a legacy so strong it endures for generations to come.

Family Financial Education Plan

Use this template to develop a structured approach to financial education for family members across generations.

1. Education Needs Assessment

For each family member, identify current financial knowledge, learning style, and priority topics:

Family Member: _____

- Current financial knowledge level: [ ] Beginner [ ] Intermediate [ ] Advanced
- Primary learning style: [ ] Reading [ ] Visual [ ] Interactive [ ] Discussion
- Priority financial topics:
    1.
    2.
    3.

[Repeat for each family member]

2. Educational Resources Identification

List appropriate resources for different age groups and topics:

Children (Ages 5-12):

- Books: _____
- Activities: _____
- Apps/Tools: _____

Teens (Ages 13-17):

- Books: _____
- Activities: _____
- Apps/Tools: _____

Young Adults (Ages 18-25):

- Books: _____
- Activities: _____
- Online Courses: _____

Adults (26+):

- Books: _____
- Courses: _____
- Professional Resources: _____

3. Structured Learning Plan

Outline specific learning objectives and activities by time period:

Monthly Family Financial Activities:

1.
2.

Quarterly Learning Objectives:

1.
2.

Annual Financial Education Milestones:

1.
2.

4. Experiential Learning Opportunities

Identify hands-on experiences to reinforce financial concepts:

For Children:

-
-

For Teens:

-
-

For Young Adults:

-
-

For Adults:

-
-

5. Progress Evaluation

Define how you'll assess financial education progress:

Knowledge Checkpoints:

-
-

Practical Application Assessments:

-
-

Celebration and Recognition:

-
-

Family Wealth Transfer Planning Worksheet

Use this worksheet to develop a comprehensive plan for transferring various forms of wealth to future generations.

1. Asset Inventory for Transfer Planning

List major assets requiring transfer planning:

Financial Assets:

- _____
    Estimated Value: $_____
- _____
    Estimated Value: $_____

Real Estate:

- _____
  Estimated Value: $_____
- _____
  Estimated Value: $_____

Business Interests:

- _____
  Estimated Value: $_____
- _____
  Estimated Value: $_____

Personal Property (with significant monetary or emotional value):

- _____
  Estimated Value: $_____
- _____
  Estimated Value: $_____

Intellectual Property:

- _____
  Estimated Value: $_____
- _____
  Estimated Value: $_____

2. Heir Readiness Assessment

For each potential heir, assess readiness for wealth transfer:

Heir: _____

- Financial knowledge: [ ] Limited [ ] Basic [ ] Substantial [ ] Advanced
- Resource management experience: [ ] Limited [ ] Basic [ ] Substantial [ ] Advanced
- Financial independence level: [ ] Dependent [ ] Partially Independent [ ] Fully Independent
- Special considerations: _____

[Repeat for each heir]

3. Transfer Timing Strategy

Indicate intended timing for various transfers:

During Lifetime:

- Assets to transfer now: _____
- Assets to transfer gradually: _____
- Triggers for accelerated transfers: _____

At Death:

- Assets for immediate transfer: _____
- Assets for staged/conditional transfer: _____
- Assets for long-term trust management: _____

4. Transfer Structure Selection

Identify appropriate structures for different assets:

Direct Transfers:

- Assets: _____
- Recipients: _____
- Timing: _____

Trust Transfers:

- Assets: _____
- Trust type: _____
- Beneficiaries: _____
- Distribution provisions: _____

Business Succession:

- Business: _____
- Succession mechanism: _____
- Timeline: _____
- Training/Preparation requirements: _____
  _____

5. Transfer Protection Mechanisms

Identify protections to preserve transferred assets:

Legal Protections:

-
-

Tax Efficiency Strategies:

-
-

Family Harmony Provisions:

-
-

6. Knowledge and Values Transfer

Plan for transferring non-financial assets:

Family History/Stories to Preserve:

-
-

Values Documentation Method:

-
-

Special Knowledge/Skills to Transfer:

-
-

Family Business Succession Planning Template

For families with business interests, use this template to create a structured succession plan.

1. Business Overview

Business Name: _____

Industry: _____

Years in Operation: _____

Annual Revenue: $ _____

Number of Employees: _____

Ownership Structure: _____

2. Succession Objectives

Primary Succession Goals (rank in order of priority, 1 being most important):

- Maintaining family control
- Maximizing financial value
- Preserving business legacy
- Providing family employment
- Creating liquidity for retirement
- Minimizing taxes and fees
- Ensuring business continuity
- Other: _____

3. Successor Identification and Development

Potential Family Successors:

- Name: _____
    - Current role in business: _____
    - Strengths relative to business needs: _____
      _____
    - Development needs: _____
      _____
    - Interest level in succession: [ ] Low [ ] Medium [ ] High

[Repeat for each potential successor]

Non-Family Succession Options:

- Key employee(s)
- Management buyout
- ESOP (Employee Stock Ownership Plan)
- External sale to strategic buyer
- External sale to financial buyer
- Liquidation

4. Ownership Transfer Mechanism

Preferred Transfer Method(s):

- Gifting (during life)
- Sale to family members
- Inheritance

- Trust transfer
- Hybrid approach: _____

Funding Mechanisms for Transfer:

- Seller financing
- Life insurance
- SBA or conventional loans
- Earn-out arrangements
- Other: _____

5. Timeline and Milestones

Preparation Phase:

- Start date: _____
- Key development activities: _____
  _____
- Readiness evaluation criteria: _____
  _____

Transition Phase:

- Anticipated start: _____
- Gradual role transitions: _____
  _____
- Authority transfer approach: _____
  _____

Completion Target:

- Final transfer date: _____

  _____

- Post-succession role of current owner(s): _____

  _____

- Contingency provisions: _____

  _____

6. Valuation and Financial Considerations

Current Business Valuation: $_____

Valuation Method Used: _____

Planned Review Frequency: _____

Financial Security Provisions for Departing Owner(s):

- Ongoing compensation arrangements: _____

  _____

- Benefits continuation: _____

  _____

- Consulting agreements: _____

  _____

- Non-compete provisions: _____

7. Communication Plan

Internal Announcement Strategy:

- Timing: _____
- Method: _____
- Key messages: _____

External Communication Plan:

- Customers: _____
- Suppliers: _____
- Lenders: _____
- Community: _____

Appendix 4: Recommended Black-Owned Financial Services And Businesses

Black-Owned Banks and Credit Unions

- **OneUnited Bank**
    - Locations: Los Angeles, Boston, Miami
    - Services: Personal and business banking, mortgages, small business loans
    - Website: www.oneunited.com

APPENDICES

- **Liberty Bank**
    - Locations: New Orleans, Baton Rouge, Kansas City, Detroit, Jackson MS
    - Services: Commercial lending, mortgages, personal banking
    - Website: www.libertybank.net
- **Citizens Trust Bank**
    - Locations: Atlanta and throughout Georgia and Alabama
    - Services: Personal and commercial banking, wealth management
    - Website: www.ctbconnect.com
- **Industrial Bank**
    - Locations: Washington DC, Maryland, New Jersey, New York
    - Services: Personal and business banking, real estate loans
    - Website: www.industrial-bank.com
- **Broadway Federal Bank**
    - Locations: Los Angeles
    - Services: Apartment lending, church lending, personal banking
    - Website: www.broadwayfederalbank.com

Black-Owned Investment Firms

- **Ariel Investments**
    - Specialty: Value investing, patient capital approach
    - Minimum Investment: Varies by fund

- Website: www.arielinvestments.com
- **Brown Capital Management**
    - Specialty: Growth equity investments
    - Minimum Investment: Varies by fund
    - Website: www.browncapital.com
- **Pugh Capital Management**
    - Specialty: Fixed income investment management
    - Minimum Investment: Institutional focus
    - Website: www.pughcapital.com
- **Williams Capital Group**
    - Specialty: Fixed income, equities, corporate finance
    - Minimum Investment: Institutional focus
    - Website: www.willcap.com
- **Fairview Capital**
    - Specialty: Private equity and venture capital
    - Minimum Investment: Institutional focus
    - Website: www.fairviewcapital.com

Black-Owned Insurance Companies

- **North Carolina Mutual Life Insurance**
    - Products: Life insurance, annuities
    - Founded: 1898 (oldest Black-owned insurance company)
    - Website: www.ncmutuallife.com
- **Atlanta Life Insurance Company**
    - Products: Life insurance, retirement planning
    - Founded: 1905
    - Website: www.atlantalife.com

- **Jackson National Life Insurance**
  - Products: Annuities, life insurance, retirement planning
  - Parent: Prudential plc
  - Website: www.jackson.com
- **Global Premier Benefits**
  - Products: Medicare supplements, final expense insurance
  - Specialty: Senior market
  - Website: www.globalpremierbenfits.com

Black-Owned Financial Advisory Firms

- **2050 Wealth Partners**
  - Specialty: Comprehensive financial planning, wealth management
  - Client Focus: Professionals, entrepreneurs
  - Website: www.2050wealth.com
- **Parkway Advisors**
  - Specialty: Wealth management, retirement planning
  - Client Focus: High-net-worth individuals, families
  - Website: www.parkwayadvisors.com
- **Biltmore Capital Advisors**
  - Specialty: Investment management, financial planning
  - Client Focus: Affluent families, business owners
  - Website: www.biltmorecap.com
- **Centurion Wealth Management**
  - Specialty: Comprehensive wealth planning
  - Client Focus: Business executives, professionals

- Website: www.centurionwealth.com

Black-Owned Real Estate Companies

- **The Peebles Corporation**
    - Specialty: Development, acquisitions, property management
    - Notable Projects: Multiple $100+ million developments
    - Website: www.peeblescorp.com
- **R. Donahue Peebles Corporation**
    - Specialty: Commercial and residential development
    - Notable Projects: Urban mixed-use developments
    - Website: www.donahuepeebles.com
- **TAG Holdings**
    - Specialty: Real estate development, acquisitions
    - Additional Services: Private equity investments
    - Website: www.tagholdings.com

Black-Owned Financial Technology Companies

- **Novae**
    - Services: Credit building, business funding, financial education
    - Founded: 2014
    - Website: www.novaemoney.com
- **First Boulevard**
    - Services: Digital banking, financial education

- Founded: 2020
- Website: www.firstboulevard.com
- **Goalsetter**
    - Services: Financial literacy app for families and kids
    - Founded: 2016
    - Website: www.goalsetter.co

APPENDIX 5: The PowerNomics Reading List

Foundational Works

- **"PowerNomics: The National Plan to Empower Black America"** by Dr. Claud Anderson A comprehensive economic development plan addressing the economic needs of Black America.
- **"Black Labor, White Wealth"** by Dr. Claud Anderson Analysis of how labor from Black Americans created wealth for white Americans.
- **"Dirty Little Secrets About Black History, Its Heroes, and Other Troublemakers"** by Dr. Claud Anderson Historical examination of little-known contributions of Black Americans.
- **"More Dirty Little Secrets About Black History, Its Heroes, and Other Troublemakers"** by Dr. Claud Anderson and Brant Anderson Continuation expanding on historical contributions and economic systems.

Historical Context

- **"The Color of Money: Black Banks and the Racial Wealth Gap"** by Mehrsa Baradaran Exploration of how Black banks have functioned within a segregated financial system.
- **"Black Wealth/White Wealth: A New Perspective on Racial Inequality"** by Melvin L. Oliver and Thomas M. Shapiro Analysis of the racial wealth gap's historical development and perpetuation.
- **"The Half Has Never Been Told: Slavery and the Making of American Capitalism"** by Edward E. Baptist Examination of how slavery built economic foundations of America.
- **"Black Wall Street: From Riot to Renaissance in Tulsa's Historic Greenwood District"** by Hannibal B. Johnson Documentation of the rise, destruction, and rebirth of a prosperous Black business district.

Contemporary Economic Analysis

- **"The Black Tax: The Cost of Being Black in America"** by Shawn Rochester Quantification of the financial cost of discrimination faced by Black Americans.
- **"Black Economics: Solutions for Economic and Community Empowerment"** by Jawanza Kunjufu Practical strategies for economic development within Black communities.
- **"Post-Traumatic Slave Syndrome: America's Legacy of Enduring Injury and Healing"** by Dr. Joy DeGruy Examination of how historical trauma impacts current economic behavior and outcomes.

- **"Our Black Year: One Family's Quest to Buy Black in America's Racially Divided Economy"** by Maggie Anderson Chronicle of one family's attempt to exclusively patronize Black businesses for a year.

Group Economics Implementation

- **"Black Dollars Matter: Teach Your Dollars How to Make More Sense"** by James Clingman Practical guide to implementing collective economics principles.
- **"Buy the Block: The Everyday Person's Guide to Building Wealth Through Real Estate"** by Rico Racosky Strategies for community-based real estate investment.
- **"Collective Courage: A History of African American Cooperative Economic Thought and Practice"** by Jessica Gordon Nembhard Historical examination of cooperative economics in Black communities.
- **"The Wealth Choice: Success Secrets of Black Millionaires"** by Dennis Kimbro Analysis of common principles among economically successful Black Americans.

Business Development and Entrepreneurship

- **"Black Business Secrets: 500 Tips, Strategies, and Resources for the African American Entrepreneur"** by Dante Lee Practical guide to Black business development and success.

- **"The Real Business of Finance"** by Kevin D. Johnson Strategies for accessing capital and managing financial growth as entrepreneurs.
- **"The Memo: What Women of Color Need to Know to Secure a Seat at the Table"** by Minda Harts Career strategies for women of color in corporate environments.
- **"Black Fortunes: The Story of the First Six African Americans Who Escaped Slavery and Became Millionaires"** by Shomari Wills Historical accounts of early Black business success stories.

Investment and Wealth Building

- **"A Different Way to Invest: Your Guide to a Better Life and a Better World"** by Freeman Roney Investment strategies focused on both financial returns and community impact.
- **"7 Steps to Success for the African-American Entrepreneur"** by Dante Lee and Jack Canfield Practical business development guide focused on Black entrepreneurship.
- **"The Five-Day Financial Makeover: A Life-Changing Journey Toward Financial Freedom"** by Erika Booker Step-by-step approach to transforming personal finances.
- **"The One Week Budget: Learn to Create Your Money Management System in 7 Days or Less!"** by Tiffany Aliche (The Budgetnista) Practical financial management system focused on simplicity and implementation.

Next Generation Education

- **"Financial Freedom: A Guide for Millennials of Color"** by Jeremiah J. Brown Wealth-building strategies specific to younger generations.
- **"Rich Dad, Poor Dad: What the Rich Teach Their Kids About Money That the Poor and Middle Class Do Not!"** by Robert T. Kiyosaki Fundamental perspectives on assets, liabilities, and financial education.
- **"The Ultimate Guide to Money Management for Minorities"** by Ryan Mack Comprehensive financial guide addressing unique challenges.
- **"Raising Black Millionaires: It's Not Just About the Money"** by Thiah Veona Muhammad Guide to developing wealth mindset and capabilities in children.

ABOUT THE AUTHORS

Ash'Cash Exantus (Ash Cash) is a banking executive, wealth educator, and entrepreneur with over 15 years of experience in the financial industry. After a successful career as a banking executive, he founded MindRight Money Management, a financial education company focused on empowering communities through financial literacy.

Ash is the author of multiple best-selling books including *"Abundance is Your Birthright," "Mind Right, Money Right,"* and *"The Wake-Up Call."* His work has been featured in major media outlets including CNBC, Fox Business, Black Enterprise, and Forbes, and he regularly appears as a financial expert on radio and television programs.

Beyond his writing and media work, Ash serves as a spiritual and financial advisor to professional athletes, entertainers, and executives, helping them build and preserve wealth while creating meaningful legacies. He holds a Bachelors in Entrepreneurship Management from the Zicklin School of Business and multiple financial certifications.

Ash combines deep financial expertise with cultural relevance, making complex wealth-building principles accessible and applicable to diverse audiences. He lives with his family in Atlanta, Georgia.

Amina Phelps is a strategic business consultant, tax expert, and wealth educator with over two decades of experience helping entrepreneurs and professionals optimize their financial strategies. After beginning her career in human resources and operations with several Fortune 500 companies, she founded HR Innovation Partners, a consulting firm specializing in people solutions, business development and financial planning for high-growth enterprises.

Amina maintains multiple professional certifications in accounting and financial planning. Her expertise spans tax optimization, business structure planning, and wealth preservation strategies with particular focus on generational wealth transfer for Black families.

Her approach combines technical expertise with practical implementation, helping clients navigate complex financial systems while building sustainable wealth.

Together with her husband Ash, they reside in Atlanta with their children, where they remain active in community economic development initiatives.

For more information on the authors and their work, visit www.hrinnovationpartner.com and www.IamAshCash.com

INDEX

A
Abundance Checklist, 8-9, 301-308
Abundance Formula
components of, 8-9, 292-293
defined, 8-9
integration of, 292-293
Abundance Mindset, 293-295
vs. scarcity thinking, 294-295
elements of, 293-294
Alternative investments, 125-126, 132
Angel investing, 135-136, 238
Asset allocation, 132-134
age-based adjustments, 133-134
goal-based adjustments, 134
market condition adjustments, 134
strategic portfolio, 132-133
Authorized users (credit), 166
Automation
investment, 143
liability reduction, 187
savings, 48-49

B

Banking system, personal, 203-208
applications of, 207-208
concept explained, 204-205
implementation of, 204-206
Black banks and credit unions, 309-310
Black-owned businesses
investment in, 238-241
supporting, 237-241
directories of, 309-313
Bonds, 127
Budget
aligned with values, 47-48
creation of, 47-48
percentage-based, 47
Business acquisition, 74-75
Business income, 63, 72-76
Business investment, 238-241
Business ownership, 72-76, 134-136
tax advantages of, 247-251
Business structures, 247-251
C-corporation, 248
LLC, 248
partnership, 249
S-corporation, 248
sole proprietorship, 247
Buy, Borrow, Die strategy, 173-174, 258-259
asset location, 258
basis management, 259
charitable integration, 259

implementation at different wealth levels, 175, 192-193
tax optimization of, 258-259

C
Capital gains, 79-81
harvesting strategy, 80-81
Cash value life insurance, 201-208
as wealth-building tool, 201-203
policy design for wealth building, 202-203
tax treatment of, 201-202
Certificates of Deposit (CDs), 67-68, 156, 158
Charitable giving, 183-184, 258-259
Charitable Remainder Trusts (CRTs), 183, 254, 271
College funding, 208
Community
bridge-building beyond, 267-270
economic empowerment of, 233-278
impact of family wealth on, 242-244
investment in, 237-241
ripple effect mechanism, 242-244
Core portfolio, 126-130
models for different risk levels, 129-130
principles of construction, 127-129
Credit
as wealth-building tool, 169-174
building from zero, 166-167
bureaus and reports, 165-166
elevating to excellent, 167-169
monitoring and disputing errors, 168
protection strategies, 176-177

recovery strategies, 177
score ranges and implications, 165
scores explained, 164-165
strategic applications, 171-174
utilization management, 167
Cryptocurrency, 125-126
Cultural capital, 243

D
Debt
consolidation, 181
emergency stabilization, 178
elimination plan, 179-180
good vs. bad, 177-178
recycling strategy, 190-191
restructuring, 180-183
settlement, 182-183
Dividend income, 69-71
investment strategies, 70
reinvestment strategy, 70-71
Dynasty trusts, 210, 254, 271

E
Emergency fund. See Freedom Fund
Estate planning, 208-210, 270-276
documents, essential, 271-272
incapacity planning, 274
specialized trust strategies, 271-273
vs. legacy planning, 269-270

INDEX

F

Factor-based investing, 145
Family
credit strategy, 177-178
education system, 276-277
financial education for, 251-254
governance documentation, 283-285
insurance strategy, 212-213
investment strategy, 143-144
legacy protection system, 283-285
liability strategy, 187-188
meeting structures, 283
tax strategy, 266-267
Financial alignment, 37-51
Financial literacy
resources for, 308-313
teaching to next generation, 274-277
Financial statement, personal, 38-40
Freedom Fund, 53-65
building systematically, 61-63
calculated amount, 56-57
maintenance system, 64-65
progressive approach, 58-59
protection of, 63-64
psychological impact, 65-66
vs. emergency fund, 55-56
where to keep, 59-61

G

Goals, financial

SMART framework for, 41-42
timeframes for, 42
Group economics, 234-237
implementation spectrum, 264-266
optimization strategies, 266-267
PowerNomics approach to, 235-237

H
Home Equity Lines of Credit (HELOCs), 172, 192, 193

I
I Bonds, 60-61
Income
broadening strategies, 63-82
characterization strategies, 260
shifting strategies, 263
stacking, 73
streams, seven types, 71-82
timing strategies, 260
Inheritance
preparation for, 276-277
sudden wealth syndrome, 276
Insurance
company selection criteria, 213-214
life. See Life insurance
ongoing management of, 215
policy design optimization, 214-215
trust ownership of, 209-210, 282
Integrated prosperity framework, 272-273
Interest income, 67-69

CD ladder strategy, 68-69
strategic sources, 67-68
Intentional spending, 44-45
International life insurance trusts (ILITs), 210, 271
Investment
advanced strategies, 144-147
alternative, 125-126
amplification, 171-172
core portfolio, 126-130
direct indexing, 146-147
factor-based, 145
implementation systems, 142-143
income strategies, 145-146
management systems, 142-143
opportunistic tactical allocation, 146
policy statements, 142
private, 134-136
real estate, 130-132
review protocols, 142
spectrum overview, 124-126
tax-loss harvesting, 144-145

J
Job security myth, 71-72

L
Legacy
capital, four dimensions of, 270
defined, 269-270
establishment of, 269-290

family protection system, 283-285
vs. estate planning, 269-270
Leverage
effect in investment returns, 139
in wealth building, 171-174, 189-190
Liabilities
diminishing, 177-195
family strategy for, 187-188
relationship with wealth, 177-178
reduction framework, 178-180
reduction systems, 186-187
true cost calculation, 178
wealth impact of reduction, 178-179
Life insurance
advanced strategies, 210-212
as wealth-building tool, 201-203
deferred compensation funding, 211
estate planning integration, 281-282
family insurance strategy, 212-213
policy selection and management, 213-215
premium financing, 211
specialized trust strategies, 210
split-dollar arrangements, 211
strategic applications, 203-204
types explained, 198-201
wealth replacement strategies, 209, 281-282
Loans. See Credit Long-term care planning, 199, 200

M
Mentorship, economic, 241-242

effective models, 241-242
for youth entrepreneurship, 242
industry-specific programs, 241
technical skill transfer, 241
Money market accounts, 60, 67-68
Mortgage refinancing, 180-181

N
Net worth statement, 39-40

O
Opportunity Zone investments, 256

P
Pay yourself first principle, 47
Permanent life insurance, 199-201
indexed universal life, 200
universal life, 199
variable universal life, 200
whole life, 199
Personal banking concept, 204-205
Portfolio
construction principles, 127-129
core models, 129-130
opportunistic, 133
strategic, 132-133
PowerNomics, 8, 74, 235-237
approach to group economics, 235-237
reading list, 313-316
Private equity, 135-136
Private investments, 134-136

Q
Qualified Personal Residence Trusts (QPRTs), 255, 272

R
Real estate
acquisition and optimization, 171-172
alternative strategies, 132
investment approaches, 130-132
professional status, 256
rental income, 76-79
rental property strategies, 77-78
tax advantages, 251-258
Retirement
account optimization, 260-261
planning, 260-261
tax strategies for, 260-261
Risk-return relationship, 123-124
Rockefeller family
approach to legacy, 277-280
principles adapted for different wealth levels, 280
Royalty income, 81-84
creator ecosystem strategy, 83-84
strategies for generating, 82-83

S
Savings
alignment with spending, 37-51
automation of, 48-49
increasing rate progressively, 62
Securities-backed lines of credit (SBLOCs), 140, 172, 193

INDEX

Self-directed IRAs, 257
Side hustle strategies, 73-74
Special Needs Trusts, 273
Spending
aligned with values, 44-46
intentional, 44-45
pay yourself first principle, 47
Spousal Lifetime Access Trusts (SLATs), 254-255
State tax planning, 264

T
Tax
avoidance vs. evasion, 247
business structures and benefits, 247-251
code as tool vs. rule, 246-247
effective planning impact, 245-246
family strategy, 266-267
healthcare strategies, 263-264
implementation systems, 265-266
income timing and characterization, 260
life insurance integration, 201-203
loss harvesting, 144-145
personal optimization, 259-264
phases of life strategy, 264-265
planning team, 265
preparation vs. strategy paradigm, 245
projection systems, 265
real estate advantages, 251-258
strategy calendar, 265
strategy evaluation metrics, 266

trust strategies, 253-255
wealth strategy, 245-267
Term life insurance, 198-199
Treasury bills and notes, 60
Trust strategies
charitable remainder trusts, 254
for tax efficiency, 253-255
implementation considerations, 254-255
intentionally defective grantor trusts, 253
jurisdictional selection, 254
qualified personal residence trusts, 255
spousal lifetime access trusts, 254-255
types for tax planning, 253-255

V
Vertical integration, 236

W
Wealth
building with life insurance, 201-203
impact of liability reduction, 178-179
mission statement, 270-272
replacement strategies, 209, 281-282
vision of abundance realized, 296
Wealth transfer planning, 280-281
worksheet for, 318-322
Wills vs. trusts, 270-271

Y
Youth
entrepreneurship development, 242

financial education for, 274-277
leadership development, 244

www.ingramcontent.com/pod-product-compliance
Lightning Source LLC
Chambersburg PA
CBHW070124080526
44586CB00015B/1549